D0616510

CHURCHES
IN COVENANT
COMMUNION
The Church of Christ Uniting

Approved and recommended to the churches
by the Seventeenth Plenary of the
Consultation on Church Union

December 9, 1988
New Orleans, Louisiana

Copies available from

Consultation on Church Union
Research Park, 151 Wall Street
Princeton, New Jersey 08540-1514

Prices in USA and Canada

1 - 9 copies	$2.00 plus postage
10 - 99 copies	$1.75 plus postage
100 - 999 copies	$1.50 plus postage
1000 copies and over	$1.25 plus postage

Copyright © Consultation on Church Union, 1989
Printed in the United States of America
ISBN 0-940186-09-8

Table of Contents

MEMBERSHIP OF THE DRAFTING COMMISSIONS

RELATED MATERIALS AND INTERPRETIVE RESOURCES

Preface

With thanksgiving to God, the Seventeenth Plenary of the Consultation on Church Union unanimously commends to the member churches the following plan for the formation under God of a covenant communion of the churches. The action of the Plenary in transmitting this document to the churches is as follows:

RESOLVED: the Seventeenth Plenary meeting of the Consultation on Church Union, assembled in New Orleans on December 5-9, 1988, approves the document, *Churches in Covenant Communion: The Church of Christ Uniting*, and commends it to the participating churches with the request that each church, by formal action,

1) approve this text as the definitive agreement for joining with other participating churches in covenant communion, including the acts sufficient to enable it,
2) declare its willingness to enter into a relationship of covenant communion with the member churches of the Consultation on Church Union and other churches which similarly approve this agreement and *The COCU Consensus* which is its theological basis, sealed by the proposed inaugural liturgies, and
3) begin to identify for itself such steps and procedures as may be necessary to prepare for the reconciliation of ordained ministries and for entering into covenant communion as set forth in this document.

The word, "definitive," as used in this resolution, has the common meaning of "that which defines" the agreement, rather than implying for it any loftier finality. The document is commended as a sufficient plan for the member churches to enter into covenant communion with one another, while anticipating that the Holy Spirit has yet more light to break upon them in their sacred journey with one another and with others who may from time to time join them on the way.

The Consultation on Church Union is composed of officially elected representatives of those churches which are committed to seek together a form of visible unity which will be at once truly catholic, truly evangelical, and truly reformed. The member churches of the Consultation on Church Union are:

>African Methodist Episcopal Church
>African Methodist Episcopal Zion Church
>Christian Church (Disciples of Christ)
>Christian Methodist Episcopal Church
>Episcopal Church
>International Council of Community Churches
>Presbyterian Church (U.S.A.)
>United Church of Christ
>United Methodist Church

Further, the Consultation has been joined in its quest by officially designated representatives of three other churches which have participated in an advisory capacity in the development of this plan, without membership in the Consultation. These "Advisory Participant" churches are:

>Evangelical Lutheran Church in America
>Reformed Church in America
>Roman Catholic Church

The National Council of Churches, through its Commission on Regional and Local Ecumenism, has been an "Advisory Participant" as well. The valuable assistance of the representatives of each of these bodies is gratefully acknowledged.

For a complete listing of the representatives who participated in the Seventeenth Plenary of the Consultation on Church Union, together with a record of the Plenary's actions in submitting this plan to the churches, the reader may wish to consult the published *Digest of the Proceedings of the Seventeenth Meeting of the Consultation on Church Union* (Volume XVII in the series of such Digests), accessible in the libraries of all the theological seminaries of the member churches of the Consultation. Additional copies may be purchased from the office of the Consultation on Church Union, 151 Wall Street, Princeton, New Jersey 08540.

>David W. A. Taylor
>General Secretary

Foreword

1) This document, together with its companion text, *The COCU Consensus*[1] issued four years earlier, constitutes a proposal for the emergence of the Church of Christ Uniting — a new ecclesial reality. It is not a new denomination, nor is it another council of churches; rather, it is a covenant communion of churches. In the Church of Christ Uniting, the richly varied cultures, traditions and institutional forms of the several churches will continue to be distinguishable. At the same time these churches will enter into a new relationship of unity in things which are essential to the church's life, namely: faith, sacraments, ministry, and mission. It is church unity in a new form — not structural consolidation, but unity in diversity among churches which, though many, are one body in Christ.

2) *The COCU Consensus*, issued in November, 1984, contains the theological basis of the covenanting proposal,[2] while the definition of the covenanting relationship and the proposed process for entering into it are set forth in this document, *Churches in Covenant Communion*, issued in December, 1988. These two texts are integrally related to each other as expressions of faith (*The COCU Consensus*) and of order (*Churches in Covenant Communion*). Together, they constitute a single proposal to the churches participating in the Consultation on Church Union. Cross references from this text to *The COCU Consensus* are intended to show the essential relationship of the two, thereby making it unnecessary to reiterate in this text the theological foundations that have been laid in the other.

3) This document (*Churches in Covenant Communion*) is composed of two parts. One is a discursive treatment of the covenanting proposal; the other consists of the liturgical texts which are intended to be used in the acts by which covenanting is to be inaugurated. Both parts are closely interrelated, and form together a single integrated text.

4) An earlier draft version of this document, entitled *Covenanting Toward Unity*, was issued in 1984 for study and response. The present

---

[1]*The COCU Consensus: In Quest of a Church of Christ Uniting*, Princeton, NJ: The Consultation on Church Union, 1985, 55 pp.

[2]For a fuller exposition of what is meant by referring to *The COCU Consensus* as "the theological basis" of the covenanting proposal, see Chapter IV, Element "1": "Claiming Our Unity in Faith," pp. 15-16.

1

text, issued in 1988, has been thoroughly revised in light of comments received from the member churches and other bodies, including a score of state and local councils of churches. The experience of oppressed persons, including especially the experience of African Americans, was brought significantly to bear upon this study through a major "Consultation on an Inclusive Church," sponsored by the COCU Commission on Racism. Insights gained from this rich variety of studies have contributed significantly to the present text.

5) Of the many changes made during the process of revising the document, the most significant has to do with the way that the goal of the covenanting process is now stated. Covenanting was described in 1984 as an interim step on the way toward becoming one church. Though appreciative of such unions in the past, the responses to the 1984 text revealed profound resistance to that expression of the goal for the Consultation. Yet paradoxically that resistance was coupled with a genuine yearning for the unity of the church. On closer examination it became apparent that what was being resisted was any commitment to an eventual merger of church structures. In the present document, therefore, all reference to the goal as an "interim step" toward something else has been removed from the text; and "church union" has been defined in a new way. In this document it implies, not consolidation of forms and structures, but what the early church referred to as "communion in sacred things." That means becoming one in faith, sacraments, ministry, and mission. This kind of unity is visible and organic, whether or not organizational structures are consolidated. In a word, it is covenant communion — a form of church unity broad enough and deep enough to permit an ever-widening circle of churches to manifest their unity in Christ. In the present understanding of the churches, the Church of Christ Uniting referred to in *The COCU Consensus* means this covenant communion.

6) This shift in focus, it must be acknowledged, appears to create some divergence between this document and portions of *The COCU Consensus*, particularly its "Foreword," at those points where either "covenanting" or the goal of covenanting is described. Inasmuch as several of the member churches have already taken formal action to approve the theological document (*The COCU Consensus*), the Consultation deems it inappropriate to reopen the 1984 theological text at this time for what would be essentially editorial emendation to bring the earlier document into conformity with the later. Instead, the Consultation on Church Union has taken the following action to reconcile the two documents:

> RESOLVED: the 17th plenary meeting of the Consultation on Church Union, assembled in New Orleans on December 5-9, 1988, declares that the revised text of *Churches in Covenant*

Communion: The Church of Christ Uniting, approved by this plenary assembly, is the statement of the Consultation concerning "covenanting," superseding all prior statements thereon. Hence, *The COCU Consensus* (1984) is hereafter to be interpreted in the light of the revised understanding of these matters set forth in the document, *Churches in Covenant Communion* (1988).

7) After twenty-eight years of patient and persistent labor by the representatives of the churches, the initial suggestion which was put forward for a new form of church union — one that would be truly catholic, truly evangelical, and truly reformed — now finds embodiment in this document, *Churches in Covenant Communion: The Church of Christ Uniting*, together with its theological basis set forth earlier and itself a part of the proposal. The Consultation on Church Union is not a permanent ecumenical agency; it is a temporary body authorized to seek a way for visible unity among the churches which constitute it. Such a way is now proposed in this document. Should the participating churches approve this proposal and inaugurate the covenant communion here described, the Consultation on Church Union will have finished its assigned task, and its responsibilities will pass to others described in this proposal. The covenant communion itself, under the leadership of its covenanting councils, will be the successor to the Consultation on Church Union.

PART I

The Covenanting Proposal

I
What Kind of Unity?

1) Scripture makes clear that Jesus calls the church to become visibly one. On the night before his crucifixion, Jesus prayed for the disciples and for those who would follow:

> "I do not pray for these only, but also for those who are to believe in me through their word, that they may all be one; even as you, Father, are in me, and I in you, that they also may be in us, so that the world may believe that you have sent me."
>
> — John 17:20-21

2) Based on the conviction, grounded in Scripture and Tradition, that God wills the unity of the church, the following proposal describes a covenantal form of unity. Biblical examples of unity are expressed in metaphor, such as Isaiah's vision of the peaceable kingdom (Isaiah 11), and in parable, such as Jesus' story of the great feast. (Luke 14) Rooted in the nature and action of the triune God, who is revealed to us as unity in diversity, the covenanting churches of the Consultation on Church Union hold to the vision of a reconciled and reconciling household of faith. Scripture and Tradition provide guidance on matters of unity, even though no blueprint exists.

3) Attentive to the yearnings and insights discerned from ecumenical dialogues over many years, the partner churches have come to believe that such a form of unity bears at least the following characteristics:[3]

(a) Celebration of God's grace will be central to our life together. (Eph. 2:12-21)

(b) Working together in Christ's mission of salvation for the whole world will mark our endeavors. (Matt. 28:18-19a)

(c) Each member, by virtue of baptism, will be understood to be a member of the apostolic and priestly ministry. (I Peter 2:9-10)

---

[3]Adapted from *The COCU Consensus*, pp. 12-14.

7

(d) The form of unity will mirror the diversity of its membership in every aspect of its fellowship and ministry. (I Cor. 12:12-27)

(e) In seeking God's justice in church and world, the reconciled communions will embody the unity that is God's gift. (Lk. 2:46-55)

(f) Because of the mutual enrichment of our several traditions, this covenantal form of unity will more faithfully reflect the universality of the body of Christ and include the strengthening of our previous ecumenical commitments. (I Cor. 1:12-17)

(g) Covenant communion assumes a new kind of ecclesial reality, an organic life that includes, in Pauline language, those "joints and ligaments" which enable the church to act as one body knit together under Christ the head. (Col. 2:19; Eph. 4:15-16)

4) Given such characteristics of the unity God wills for the church, the Consultation on Church Union calls upon its member churches to confess their complicity in the sin of the church's division, and to do all that can be done to exhibit that unity. Moreover, the Consultation proposes to the member churches, in the pages that follow, a form of unity which it believes to be at once faithful to God's will, appropriate to the present circumstances, and open to the future for renewal and reformation. It is a proposal which calls for unity of heart and mind, for unity in faith, in prayer, in the breaking of bread, in the Word of the gospel, in ministry, in sharing, and in witness and service to the world. (Acts 2:42-44) Such unity will be a visible witness to the world of God's saving power in Jesus Christ. The Consultation on Church Union calls the churches to communion in Christ — a covenantal communion in faith, sacraments, ministry, and mission. The name here given to the churches in covenant communion is **The Church of Christ Uniting**, and the means by which it comes into being is referred to as "covenanting."

II
What Is Covenanting?

1) "Covenanting," as the Consultation uses the term, is both an act and a process by which the churches come into a new relationship with one other.

2) It is an *act* of covenant by churches which, though one in Christ, are currently divided from one another. By this solemn act the churches will commit themselves, before God and each other, to live henceforth in one covenantal communion even though they continue to exist as distinct ecclesiastical systems.

3) Such a covenantal act will inaugurate also a *process* of deepening commitment by these churches to one another in which the Spirit's gift of unity in Christ will be enabled to grow and to flower. The process will be one of maturing in unity as the covenanting churches jointly identify and take such mutually agreed actions as may serve to deepen their communion in faith, sacrament, ministry, and mission.

4) In covenanting, diversities remain even while the covenanting partners become truly one. Moreover covenant communion is itself a way of *being* one. The church is by its very nature a pilgrim people. Through covenant communion the relationship with one another will grow, deepen, and change as it matures over the years, as this covenant communion is drawn forward by the Holy Spirit into the fullness of God's perfect will for the church.

5) In covenant communion the churches may maintain, for so long as each may determine, their own church structures and traditions, including present forms of worship, systems of ministerial selection, training, and placement, their international, confessional, and communion relationships, and their mission programs.[4] What covenanting means is that these now separated churches will resolve to live as one in the most basic things — in faith, sacrament, ministry, and mission. Uniformity in structure is not essential to covenant communion.

6) Approaching Christian unity in this way will tend to focus the energy of the churches' shared life upon the local communities of now

---

[4]*The COCU Consensus:* pg. 11, par. 4; also pp. 13-14, par. 6(e) and 6(f).

separated congregations. For it is in such towns, neighborhoods, and local areas that Christians most often gather about the Word and sacraments, served by their recognized ministers, in living communities of faith and mission. Covenanting will make it possible for these several congregations in each place to see themselves not only as members of a particular communion but also as members of a living and functioning communion of communions, sharing the one baptism, proclaiming the one faith, receiving together the one bread and cup, recognizing the ministry of each as a ministry to all, and reaching out as one in love and service to the world.

7) A covenant communion of churches is, by definition, committed to become truly inclusive. Each partner is enriched by sharing in the gifts that God has given to the other. Each partner works to take down walls of alienation that exist between the churches, and to overcome attitudes which tend to marginalize persons in regard to race, class, age, gender, disabilities, marital status, sexual orientation, and positions of power and powerlessness, and to live toward a church in which all participate in the wholeness of Christ.

8) In covenanting, the churches will make an act of common repentance for the sin of disunity among them, and for the sins which inhibit community within the human family.[5] In living out that repentance, the covenanting churches dare to believe that in sacramental communion these sins can be faced in a substantially new way. What is needed for reconciliation is a new and intentional community of the Spirit, rooted in one Lord, one faith, one baptism, and nurtured at one eucharistic table. Such unity anticipates God's coming future, now unfolding in Jesus Christ. It is the promised gift of the Holy Spirit to those who penitently ask for it and diligently seek it.

9) Covenant communion is intended to be a sign and foretaste of the community God wills for the world. In its ultimate intent, it is for the salvation of each and all. It is for the redemption of the world.

---

[5]See pp. 47-48 ("A National Service for Declaring Covenant . . . "), the Prayer of Confession on the first and second pages of this liturgy.

III
How To Initiate Covenanting

1) Faithfulness to God's mission in the world impels the member churches to enter into covenanting. To initiate covenanting, actions of several different kinds will be required. Just as doctrine, polity, and liturgy are basic to the church's life and mission, so also the initiation of covenanting has these same three interrelated dimensions:
— *Theological*: the churches receive and voice together the faith of the church through the ages.
— *Governmental*: the governing bodies of the church consider and act on commonly developed proposals for Christian unity.
— *Liturgical*: the churches' unity is declared and confirmed in corporate acts of worship.

To initiate covenanting, action in all three of these dimensions is required, in faith that it is God who moves the churches to act and who alone is able to sustain them in covenant communion. In Christ, the interrelationship between these three dimensions can be discerned: the church's theological *affirmation* is grounded in the joyful praise of God, with implications for the church's polity; its governmental *decision* has a theological grounding, with implications for the church's worship; and its liturgical *action* has a grounding in the church's polity, with implications for the church's theology.

2) **The theological dimension** of entering into covenanting is basic to the rest. The Consultation on Church Union has looked carefully at the differences which historically have divided the several traditions. Through the consultative process, confirmed by the claiming of *The COCU Consensus*, the churches have come to recognize in one another the apostolic faith of the church universal: the Tradition.[6] Through covenanting, the distinctive treasures of these several histories will be maintained, while their insights and emphases will be made increasingly accessible to others for the common good. The process of covenanting begins by joyfully affirming the Christian faith.

---

[6]*The Cocu Consensus*, pg. 30, par. 6-7.

3) **The governmental dimension** of entering into covenanting is also essential. This has to do with the decision making processes of each church. It includes voting. For the church, however, voting is much more than an exercise of democratic rule. When Christians gather in church governing bodies and seek God's leading through prayer and careful listening to one another in faith, God is there in the midst of them. The formal decision by each church to enter into this new relationship is therefore much more than a preparation for covenanting, but is itself a dimension of covenanting. Such governing action by each church is, the Consultation believes, a manifestation of God's action through the Holy Spirit in drawing the churches together into covenant communion.

4) **The liturgical dimension** of entering into covenanting is crucial as well. It is God who effects reconciliation in the divided household of faith. Corporate expressions of mutual commitment, shared hope, and common will must therefore be lifted up together in words and actions appropriate to the worship of God. Agreements reached separately must be celebrated together. The liturgical action in covenanting is much more than a ceremonial capstone for a uniting covenant which has been successfully voted; the liturgical action itself will be a sign and means of church unity.

5) Each of these dimensions has both an internal and an external aspect, related respectively to the church's life and to its mission. Thus the church's *doctrinal* life, consisting in appropriation of apostolic faith through continual theological reflection and teaching, finds its missional aspect in the urgent proclamation of the gospel of Jesus Christ, by word and deed, in and to the world. Similarly, the church's *polity* as the pastoral pattern of its life in Christ at once stands under the constant judgment of the gospel of God's reign and is directed to active mission for a just and life-giving stewardship of creation. Also, the *worship* of God in the church's life issues in mission and service to the whole human community created in the divine image and redeemed by Christ from its multiple distortions. Mission illuminates each of these three dimensions.

6) Crucial to covenant communion, in all three of the dimensions by which it is initiated, is a deliberate process of reception of the covenanting agreements by the churches. Such reception includes the participation and nurture of the people of the church, enabling them to understand and to receive these agreements and to enter fully the covenant communion into which their churches are being drawn. No such communion is possible, whatever one's system of church government may be, without the willing and joyful assent of the people of God. To that end, it is essential that the membership of the churches

be fully informed about what is being proposed, so that their AMEN may be from the heart. A strong educational effort, accompanied by relationships which anticipate covenant life, can be an important part of the reception process. These can serve as vehicles of the Holy Spirit for building and strengthening ecclesial communion, as the churches find themselves increasingly beckoned of God to be and become one covenant people in Christ.

IV
The Elements Of Covenanting

1) Since the unity that we seek is not chiefly organizational, what then are the identifying characteristics of that covenant communion here described? Through the Consultation on Church Union, the participating churches have together identified eight elements of covenanting, none of which now consistently characterize the relationship between these churches. They are:

1. claiming unity in faith;
2. commitment to seek unity with wholeness;
3. mutual recognition of members in one baptism;
4. mutual recognition of each other as churches;
5. mutual recognition and reconciliation of ordained ministry;
6. celebrating the Eucharist together;
7. engaging together in Christ's mission;
8. formation of covenanting councils.

These are described more fully below. They are called "elements" because each is regarded as basic to a covenant communion of churches. Together, they comprise a single reality, and each in its own way is essential to the whole.

Claiming Our Unity in Faith

> There is one body and one Spirit, just as you were called to the one hope that belongs to your call, one Lord, one faith, one baptism, one God and Father of us all, who is above all and through all and in all.
> — Ephesians 4:4-6

2) The "one faith" which the church proclaims and by which it lives is the faith of the one holy catholic and apostolic church. This is the faith to which Scripture and Tradition bear witness. Notwithstanding differences of emphasis and interpretation, the covenanting churches dare to affirm their essential unity in the faith. Claiming that faith in common is basic to covenant communion.

3) The ancient ecumenical creeds are not only witnesses to the

faith but also abiding symbols[7] of that faith. The divided voices of many churches, however, make it difficult today for the faith of the church to be heard by all as one. After more than two decades of theological work by officially designated persons responsible to the most authoritative bodies in the several churches, it is now evident that an essential core of theological agreement exists and continues to grow among these churches in matters of faith, worship, sacrament, membership, ministry, and mission. That agreement is expressed in *The COCU Consensus: In Quest of a Church of Christ Uniting* (1984). The existence of that document is a sign of these churches' basic unity in faith; their claiming of it is treated as an element of covenanting.

4) *The COCU Consensus* is not a complete exposition of every article of Christian doctrine. It is intended rather as a *sufficient* expression of the apostolic faith, order, worship, and witness to enable the participating churches to enter together into a covenanting relationship. It also is intended as the theological foundation for the vision of a covenant communion of communions which these churches seek by God's grace to become. It is therefore the theological basis of the document in hand, *Churches in Covenant Communion: The Church of Christ Uniting*. For a fuller expression of what it means to "claim" the consensus, see the Foreword of *The COCU Consensus*, pages 2-3.

Commitment to Seek Unity with Wholeness

5) Commitment to Christian unity is essential if churches are to become visibly one. The Consultation affirms that unity is a gift of God, to be made visible among the churches in response to the prayers and actions of those who diligently seek it.

6) Through patient and persistent work over many years, the covenanting churches have been led by God to overcome seemingly insurmountable obstacles to unity in matters of faith, sacraments, ministry, and mission. For this the church gives thanks to God. Yet the churches still are not one in other ways. Racism and sexism still live as idolatries in churches, continuing to divide and destroy. Handicapism marginalizes people with disabilities as the institutions of both church and society continue to value physical wholeness in divisive and destructive ways. Rich and poor seldom worship God together. These are theological issues, just as truly as those of sacrament and mission,

---

[7]The original meaning of "symbol" is: "an authoritative summary of faith or doctrine." For centuries it has been used in this way to refer to the creeds of the church. Other meanings of the word, such as a token or arbitrary sign, are of more recent development. The word derives from Greek (*syn* + *ballein*) meaning literally to "cast together" — that is, to hold two things side by side for comparison, as proof of authenticity.

for they demonstrate to the world the church's disobedience to the will of Christ "that they may all be one."[8]

7) Commitment to a living unity, therefore, requires a change of heart — "transformed by the renewal of your mind"[9] — not for the sake of the church alone, but ultimately for the sake of that larger oneness for which our Savior prays. To repent of sins that divide Christ's body is to turn from them to God, committed by God's grace to obey the clear will of Christ. It means being ready to change, especially in these idolatries which alienate and cause pain to sisters and brothers in Christ. It is to seek a unity that is inclusive of all who are baptized into Christ, while rejoicing in the diversity of persons and gifts which the Spirit has given to the church.[10]

8) **In Christ "there is neither Jew nor Greek."** God abhors racism. It is essential to Christian unity that there be a redress of racism and a commitment to racial inclusiveness, both in our churches and our society. This is not alone a matter of justice or mission. This commitment is fundamental to Christian community itself, for the church is continually called to be and to become one living communion in Christ.

9) **In Christ "there is neither bond nor free."** God abhors all forms of oppression, whether it is economic oppression or that of society's exclusion of persons with disabilities. In a community where any enrich themselves at the expense of the poor, or exert power through the disadvantage of others, Christian unity cannot exist. The gospel which the church proclaims is "good news to the poor . . . release to the captives . . . recovery of sight to the blind . . . liberty to those who are oppressed."[11] Inclusiveness is not just a matter of goodwill, but of the justice which the gospel demands. It is therefore of the very nature of the church, which is called to be one living body in Christ.

10) **In Christ "there is neither male nor female."** God abhors sexism. Degradation or diminution of others on the basis of gender, whether intended or not, is an affront to them and an offense to their Creator. The church often has fostered attitudes which devalue women. Such attitudes are the root cause of many evils which the church deplores, such as domestic violence, pornography, and the disproportionate poverty of women. Opportunities for leadership and full partici-

---

[8]*The COCU Consensus*, pp. 9-10, par. 16.

[9]Romans 12:2.

[10]"For as many of you as were baptized into Christ have put on Christ. There is neither Jew nor Greek, there is neither bond nor free, there is neither male nor female; for you are all one in Christ Jesus." (Galatians 3:27-28)

[11]Luke 4:18.

pation in the church are in many instances still effectively closed to women. The church cannot be whole without the gifts both of women and men in covenant communion through Christ.

11) Inclusiveness is essential to Christian unity. The word "inclusive," however, must be used with some care. For example, ethnic minorities often hear the word as a patronizing invitation to become part of the dominant group — to enter another's reality, but one which the other continues to dominate. And gay and lesbian persons in most churches seldom are included at all, if they are open in acknowledging their sexual identity. The appeal to inclusiveness is heard by some as an invitation to give up one's distinctive identity and merge into a culture alien to one's own. So the word "inclusive" is not an altogether adequate word, though it is far better than any others that have yet been proposed to replace it. The Consultation uses it, therefore, sensitive to its possible misuse, being deeply persuaded that there can be no unity for the church unless it is truly inclusive. By "inclusiveness" is meant the catholicity of God's inclusiveness.

12) The goal of this covenant communion is not a homogenization of all differences into a new sameness, but a new community in Christ, in which differences are affirmed, accepted, and celebrated as the gifts of God for the common good. This is a work of divine grace. The integrity, moral authority, and strength of witness that this covenant communion of churches will have within the nation and the world will be in significant measure related to its becoming, by God's grace, a truly inclusive communion in Christ.

Mutual Recognition of Members in One Baptism

13) Scripture and Tradition are united in witness that there is one baptism with water in the name of the triune God. Baptismal practice among the churches, however, is quite diverse, including both a variety of baptismal modes and, for some, preliminary acts of dedication or blessing and, for others, additional acts of affirmation of baptismal vows such as confirmation. [12] This diversity reflects not different baptisms but different facets of the one baptism into the one body of the one Lord. [13] (Eph. 4:4-6)

14) At its 1974 plenary session the Consultation on Church Union proposed a "Mutual Recognition of Members," by which it invited the member churches to recognize that "all who are baptized into Christ

---

[12]The rite of confirmation is addressed under the heading of the renewal of baptismal vows in *The COCU Consensus*, page 37, par. 13-14. See also the document, *An Order for an Affirmation of the Baptismal Covenant (Also Called Confirmation)*, produced by the Consultation on Church Union and available from its office.

[13]*The COCU Consensus*, pg. 37, par. 11.

are members of Christ's universal church and belong to and share in Christ's ministry through the people of the one God, Father, Son, and Holy Spirit." Over the next four years each of the participating churches took formal and official action approving this resolution. These acts were a dramatic witness to our unity in Christ.

15) In its 1979 plenary, the Consultation proposed to its member churches that each take actions to move "Beyond Affirmation to Action" in implementing such mutual recognition. Many suggestions were offered by the plenary, and a number of significant actions were taken in response by the several churches, but much remains to be done. Recovery of our unity in baptism is at the heart of the covenanting journey, for it is central to realization of genuine *koinonia* among the churches.[14] Mutual recognition of members in one baptism is of basic ecclesiological significance. It implies recognition of the ministry of all the others in the common priesthood in which and from which God calls those ministers who will be ordained. Membership in Christ and in Christ's church is for every believer a calling by God to ministry and witness in the world.[15]

Mutual Recognition of Each Other as Churches

16) A church's membership in the Consultation on Church Union implies at least *some recognition* of the other member churches as participants in the one church of Jesus Christ. So, also does membership in a council of churches. In local experience, congregations have sometimes achieved relationships which amount to mutual recognition in spite of certain canons and constitutions of their churches. The fact is, however, that the member churches of the Consultation on Church Union, acting in conformity with their respective foundational documents and theological principles, have not yet recognized each other as churches truly catholic, truly evangelical, and truly reformed. The absence of mutual recognition comes as a surprise to many who have been unaware of the official positions of the churches, and compels us to press on until such mutual recognition is achieved.

17) Covenanting provides the occasion and the means whereby that which is implicit in the relationship among the churches may become explicit, that which is privately and unofficially acknowledged may be openly and joyfully declared before God and many witnesses. To that end, in the liturgical event in which covenanting is inaugurated, participating churches through their authorized representatives will together make affirmations of:

---

[14]*The COCU Consensus*, pp. 36-37, par. 10.

[15]*The COCU Consensus*, pg. 42, par. 21; also pg. 43, par. 24.

— faith in the one God who through the Word and in the Spirit creates, redeems, and sanctifies;

— commitment to Jesus Christ as Savior and as the incarnate and risen Lord;

— obedience to the Holy Scriptures which testify to Tradition and to which Tradition testifies, as containing all things necessary for our salvation as well as being the rule and ultimate standard of faith;

— commitment to faithful participation in the two sacraments ordained by Jesus Christ, baptism and the Lord's Supper;

— commitment to the evangelical and prophetic mission of God and to God's reign of justice and peace;

— grateful acceptance of the ministry which the Holy Spirit has manifestly given to the churches.

These affirmations are to be voiced together in the liturgical act by which covenanting will be inaugurated. [16] Through these words spoken together, each church will publicly and officially recognize the others as authentic expressions of the one, holy, catholic, and apostolic church of Jesus Christ. This liturgical action will fulfill the intention to confess the faith together affirmed in Chapter V of *The COCU Consensus*, where the fundamental sources of the doctrine of the faith are described in detail: Scripture, Tradition, and the creeds and confessions of the church, together with worship, mission, and inclusiveness as forms of confession.

Mutual Recognition and Reconciliation of Ordained Ministry

18) Through their baptism all Christians are called and empowered by the Holy Spirit to share in the ministry of Jesus Christ in the church and in the world. [17] Those among them who are ordained to particular ministries share also in that common ministry of the people of God, and represent to every member the ministry of Christ to which all have been called. [18] Because the ministry of the baptized is affirmed already by each of the covenanting churches, there appears to be no impediment to public recognition and reconciliation of this common ministry. Obstacles remain to be overcome, however, to effect the mutual recognition and reconciliation of our ordained ministries. In the paragraphs which follow, therefore, attention is focused largely upon the ordained

---

[16]See pg. 53.

[17]*The COCU Consensus*, pp. 43-44, par. 24-25. See also *Baptism, Eucharist, and Ministry* (Faith and Order paper no. 111), Geneva: World Council of Churches, 1982: "Ministry," sections I and II.

[18]*The COCU Consensus*, pg. 45-46, par. 27-31.

because that is where obstacles to the mutual recognition and reconciliation of our ministries lie.

19) The theological understanding of ministry, both lay and ordained, which underlies covenanting is set forth in Chapter VII of *The COCU Consensus*. But it is important to remember how that chapter of the Consensus is intended to function in the covenanting process. It is not a constitution.

> Many details are deliberately left unsettled. There is room for the participating churches to grow together in unforeseen ways as they work out the implications of the covenant.[19]

In the realm of ministerial order, just as in the doctrines of the faith, there is a historic tradition which these churches hold in common, despite their differing expressions of it; and it is this that the Consultation has sought to express in Chapter VII of *The COCU Consensus*. The concept of ministry expressed there is not embodied in quite this way in any of the participating churches. Yet there can be seen in the divergent polities of the member churches particular ministries which are in fact episcopal, presbyteral, diaconal, and lay in their essential nature. Chapter VII articulates this historic, underlying pattern, providing thereby a common frame of reference for recognizing in one another's ministries the ministry of the church through the ages, and thus for reconciling their ministries one to another. Uniformity among the several church polities is not essential to covenant communion; but mutual recognition and reconciliation of the ordained ministries is essential, for it is integrally related to the recognition of churches.

20) Mutual *recognition* of ordained ministries is intended to acknowledge in these ministries the manifest blessing of God and the fruit of the Spirit, and to affirm that they are rooted in the apostolic tradition.[20] Such recognition does not obscure real differences, but neither does it depend upon first setting those differences aright according to one's own tradition before recognition can be granted. To the contrary, the mutual recognition of ordained ministries is a way of acknowledging both the headship of Christ over every ecclesial tradition and the freedom of the Spirit to work in and through these traditions however the Spirit wills.

21) *Reconciliation* of ordained ministries is intended to refer to actions by the churches, both separately and together, whereby the ordained ministries of each covenanting church become one ministry of Jesus Christ in relation to all. This is not intended to mean that the

---

[19]From "A Note on the Function of Chapter VII in the Covenanting Process," *The COCU Consensus*, p. 39.

[20]*The COCU Consensus*, pp. 48-49, par. 47. See also *Baptism, Eucharist, and Ministry*, "Ministry," par. 34 and 37-38.

standard of ministerial training and certification must become the same for all the churches, nor that their call or appointment systems must change, but rather that the ministry of one may function, whenever invited, as a ministry to all. This is not now possible among all of the covenanting churches. Hence, covenanting will make possible an enrichment of the ordained ministry for each church, as well as provide a new and visible demonstration of our essential unity in faith, sacraments, ministry, and mission.

22) The method by which the covenanting churches intend to accomplish reconciliation of ordained ministries is, first, by setting this reconciliation in the context of mutual recognition of members in one baptism, mutual recognition of churches, and mutual recognition of ministries. Within the covenanting liturgy, these three acts will precede the reconciliation of ordained ministries and, taken together, are regarded as foundational to it. For the sake of reconciliation, the sequential order of these acts is important, and their close conjunction with one another is equally important. This ordering is reflected in the accompanying liturgy for declaring covenant and reconciling ordained ministers.[21] Reconciliation of ministries enables full eucharistic sharing.

23) Having mutually recognized one another's ministries, these ministers will then offer themselves in mutual commitment to one another, so that their ministry in the wider covenant communion may be received and appropriately ordered in all of the covenanting churches. To this end, the accompanying liturgies provide that the reconciliation of bishops shall include words of mutual commitment to one another in covenant, and an act of mutually laying hands upon each other in acknowledgment of the authority of the other churches within which each will, from time to time, exercise elements of shared ministry through covenanting. So also, the accompanying liturgy for the reconciliation of presbyters and welcoming of deacons includes words which similarly acknowledge the authority of the other churches within which each is enabled to minister occasionally through covenant communion, and an act of laying on of hands by a reconciled minister *of episkopé*, together with other signs of reconciliation and peace.[22]

24) Lest there be any misunderstanding in regard to the sign of reconciliation which these liturgies employ — the laying on of hands by an authorized minister of oversight — the covenanting churches recognize and declare that these are not liturgies of ordination or reordination, but of reconciliation among those whose ordained ministry already has been mutually recognized. The act of laying on hands is

---

[21]See pp. 51-54 and 56-60.

[22]See the accompanying liturgies, pp. 56-58, 58-60, and 60-63. For the meaning of *episkopé*, see *The COCU Consensus*, pp. 48-49, paragraphs 46 and 47.

used for many different purposes within the church. It is used in blessing, in confirmation, in dedication, in anointing the sick, in commissioning to tasks of education or of mission, as well as in ordination. In each case, it is the context which defines its purpose. In the covenanting liturgies, the laying on of hands is administered in silence. The context, especially the prayer which precedes or follows, leaves no doubt as to its meaning: it is an act of reconciliation.[23]

25) The Consultation is persuaded that no other sign serves that purpose as well as the ancient sign of the laying on of hands by the churches' authorized ministers of oversight. From the beginning of their journey together, the covenanting churches have sought a distinctively new communion: one that is simultaneously catholic, evangelical, and reformed. However evangelical and reformed this covenant communion may be, it will not effectively invite recognition of its ordained ministries by all parts of the universal church if the reconciliation of ordained ministries does not include the historic sign of episcopal succession — the laying on of hands. Its use under the circumstances here defined has to do, not with ordination, but with the recovery of a visible and widely valued sign of unity and continuity within the church of God, a sign that in this case signifies the mutual sharing of our ordered ministries. This understanding is in harmony with increasingly universal ecumenical understanding.[24]

26) Just as the use of this sign is judged to be essential, so also the way it is used is equally essential: by the mutual laying on of hands. It is in the mutuality of this act that each tradition gives to the other a sign of acceptance and of deepened or enriched understandings of ordination and *episkopé* as they have been preserved and practiced in the separate churches.

27) When reconciliation of ordained ministries has been achieved at the regional level,[25] everyone who is ordained thereafter in that

---

[23]See pp. 58, 60, and 62-63.

[24]*Baptism, Eucharist, and Ministry*, "Ministry" paragrph 53: "In order to achieve mutual recognition, different steps are required of different churches. For example:

a) Churches which have preserved the episcopal succession are asked to recognize both the apostolic content of the ordained ministry which exists in churches which have not matintained such succession and also the existence in these churches of a ministry of *episkopé* in various forms.

b) Churches without the episcopal succession, and living in faithful continuity with the apostolic faith and mission, have a ministry of Word and sacrament, as is evident from the belief, practice, and life of those churches. These churches are asked to realize that the continuity with the Church of the apostles finds profound expression in the successive laying on of hands by bishops and that, though they may not lack the continuity of the apostolic tradition, this sign will strengthen and deepen that continuity. They may need to recover the sign of the episcopal succession."

[25]This refers to that level of ecclesiastical jurisdiction where ordination to ministry occurs, variously described as the diocese, presbytery, region, conference, or association. (See also footnote #42 on page 31).

region will be ordained into an already reconciled ministry. No further act will be required to accomplish reconciliation. Nonetheless, the ordination of women and men to the ministry is such a highly visible act in the life of the churches that it provides for our covenant communion an unparalleled opportunity to demonstrate before the church and the world the unity which God has given. From the date of inauguration of covenant communion, there will be no more ordinations carried out in denominational isolation from the other covenanting churches. The Covenanting Councils[26] will enable the conduct of all ordination of persons, credentialed by the churches, through the laying on of hands and prayer by reconciled bishops together with the presence and participation of ministers, both lay and ordained, from as many of the covenanting churches as possible. Moreover, it is the desire of the covenanting churches that these ordinations be conducted according to mutually acceptable rites, in order to facilitate participation from all parts of the covenant communion.[27]

28) All of the participating churches in COCU already have a ministry of Word and sacrament, but not all now have a personalized ministry of *episkopé* at the middle judicatory level where ordination and pastoral care of pastors is lodged. Nor do all now have a regularly constituted office of deacon. It will be the responsibility of each participating church, prior to the COCU liturgy in which covenant is declared and ministries are reconciled, to determine how its present categories of ordained ministry relate to the historic categories set forth in *The COCU Consensus*, Chapter VII.[28]

29) Among the several functions of deacons listed in paragraph VII.63 of *The COCU Consensus*, the one function which may be regarded as *sine qua non* in identifying persons who are to be put forward initially for reconciliation as deacons is: "(f) Servants in Pastoral Care." Among the several functions of presbyters listed in *The COCU Consensus* VII.56, those which may be regarded as *sine qua non* in identifying persons who are to be put forward initially for reconciliation as presbyters are: "(a) Preachers of the Word," and "(b) Celebrants of the Sacraments." Among the several functions of bishops listed in paragraph VII.51 of *The COCU Consensus*, those which may be regarded as *sine qua non* in identifying those who are to be put

---

[26]Covenanting Councils are described later, on pp. 29ff.

[27]The phrase, "mutually acceptable rites," refers to the existing ordination rites of the covenanting churches, adapted if necessary to facilitate the full and willing participation of representative ministers from other covenanting churches in the ordination rite of one's own church. The phrase is not meant to imply the necessity of a common ordinal for the churches, nor is it meant to foreclose the possibility that the churches may wish at some time to develop together such a common rite.

[28]*The COCU Consensus*, pg. 47-48, par. 39-44.

forward initially for reconciliation as bishops are: "(c) Pastoral Overseers" of districts or regions,"[29] (e) Representative Ministers in the Act of Ordination,"[30] and "(g) Servants of the Unity of the Church."

30) Each covenanting church may find these ministerial offices already existing within its polity, or may make amendment of existing offices to the extent necessary to fulfill the intention of ministry reconciliation through covenanting, or may create a new office within the integrity of its continuing polity but in a manner conformable to the intention of ministry reconciliation through covenanting. Each church may assign or continue to use such names for these offices as it may desire; however, in the shared life of the churches they commonly will be identified as deacons, presbyters, and bishops of the covenant communion of the churches.[31]

31) By reconciliation through covenanting, a presbyter or bishop does not acquire new rights, powers, or authority within his or her own denomination or communion. Such decisions about authority are properly left to the member churches. Rather, through ministry reconciliation it becomes possible to act in ecclesial unity with other lay and ordained ministries of the covenanting churches to make manifest in new and wider ways the visible and organic unity of the church.

Celebrating the Eucharist Together

32) The Lord's Supper is the sacred feast of the people of God. In communion with Christ, members of the church are renewed in their communion with one another in Christ, and are commissioned afresh to be Christ's agents of reconciliation in the world. The sacrament is at the heart of the church's life. Regular celebration of the Eucharist

---

[27]The phrase, "mutually acceptable rites," refers to the existing ordination rites of the covenanting churches, adapted if necessary to facilitate the full and willing participation of representative ministers from other covenanting churches in the ordination rite of one's own church. The phrase is not meant to imply the necessity of a common ordinal for the churches, nor is it meant to foreclose the possibility that the churches may wish at some time to develop together such a common rite.

[28]*The COCU Consensus*, pp. 47-48, par. 39-44.

[29]The ministry of bishops as preachers of the Word and celebrants of the sacraments is included under the heading of "Pastoral Overseers" in the indicated paragraph of *The COCU Consensus*.

[30]In *The COCU Consensus*, p. 50, par. 51(e) (which refers to bishops as "Representative Ministers in the Act of Ordination"), the statement that "bishops preside at ordinations" is understood by the covenanting churches to imply (1) the personal leadership of the bishop, (2) the direct participation of the bishop in the laying on of hands, and (3) the participation of others in the act of ordination (p. 47, par. 37).

[31]*The COCU Consensus*, pp. 47-48, par. 42.

together is at the heart of covenanting as well.[32]

33) Observance of the Lord's Supper is a sign of the church's unity in Christ. In the present divided state of the churches, it is an ironic witness against their disunity as well. As Christians gather in all their diversity at one Table of the Lord, they give evidence that their communion is with Christ, and hence that they are in communion with one another in Christ. But when Christians are unable or unwilling to partake together of the one Eucharist, they witness against themselves and give a visible demonstration of the brokenness of Christ's body. Common celebration of Holy Communion is essential to the unity we seek.

34) The sacrament of the Lord's Supper exhibits a richness of meaning that is larger than the tradition of any single church. Its essential meaning is briefly stated in *The COCU Consensus*, Chapter VI, paragraphs 15-19. Without obscuring differences which remain, the covenanting churches find in *The COCU Consensus* sufficient agreement regarding the meaning of the Lord's Supper to enable partaking of it as one, while allowing for diversity of administration and practice. At the same time, they share in an increasingly universal convergence of Christian understanding that includes the following elements which should characterize all eucharistic liturgies:

— it is a great *thanksgiving* to God for everything accomplished in creation and redemption;

— it is a *memorial* of the crucified and risen Christ and a sign of Christ's redeeming love for all humankind;

— it is an *invocation* of the Holy Spirit who makes the crucified and risen Christ really present to us in the sacramental meal;

— it is a *communion* of the faithful who, in communion with Christ, are in communion with one another in Christ;

— it is a *meal* of the kingdom, a foretaste of the final redemption of all things in Christ.[33]

The eucharistic liturgies already authorized by the churches of the Consultation reflect such a mutually accepted pattern.

35) Shared celebration of the Eucharist is both a sign and a means of unity in Christ.[34] Even before the inauguration of covenanting, the churches' experience of interim eucharistic fellowship over more than a decade has demonstrated the dynamism of regular eucharistic sharing

---

[32]It is understood that every reference to the sacrament in this document implies its inseparable connection with the reading and preaching of the Word. See *The COCU Consensus*, p. 36, par 8; also p. 37, par. 15.

[33]*Baptism, Eucharist, and Ministry*, "Eucharist" II.2-26.

[34]*The COCU Consensus*, p. 37, par. 15.

for the sake of Christian unity.[35] The power of reconciling grace made present in the sacrament has been compelling in furthering a new degree of unity between churches which have been deeply separated for many years along racial lines. It is that same power which has long been evident at the Lord's Table within each church, effecting the reconciliation of those who have become personally, politically, or theologically estranged from one another.

36) The Lord's Supper also is a powerful centering reality for the church's mission. The church always is tempted to pursue either institutional or ideological ends in mission, substituting its own will for the will of Christ. Some even regard Christian unity as an enemy of the church's mission, in the belief that unity draws energy away from cherished causes. But at the eucharistic table, we "show forth the Lord's death until he comes." That is in itself a powerful act of gospel proclamation, providing the spring for Christian witness and action. Indeed, it is the paradigm of all that the church is called to say and to do in mission in the world. Unity and mission are one at the Lord's Table.

37) In covenanting, it is important that common celebrations of the Eucharist be planned with intentional regularity. The frequency of such occasions is left to the discretion of the covenanting partners in each place.

Engaging Together in Christ's Mission

38) Mission is essential to the church's apostolicity. The church is apostolic not only because it continues in the faith and teaching of the apostles, but also because it is sent, like the apostles, to carry out Christ's mission to all people. Mission is essential to life in the church. It is essential as well to life in covenant communion among the churches.

39) The mission of the church takes many forms. In simplest terms, it is a mission of reconciliation and redemption. It is participation as a commissioned servant in God's mission, which is "to unite all things in Christ, things in heaven and things on earth." (Eph. 1:10) The church engages in mission through *worship*, through *proclamation* of the gospel, and through *action* which embodies God's justice, peace and love.

40) **In worship**, the church recalls and celebrates the mighty acts of God in creation, redemption and providence; is graciously forgiven and renewed in faith, hope and love; and is sent out in the power of the Holy Spirit, individually and collectively, to be ambassadors, wit-

---

[35]*Guidelines for Interim Eucharistic Fellowship.* Princeton, NJ: Consultation on Church Union, 1973. 11p. (A useful resource offering suggestions and liturgical guidelines for shared celebrations of the Eucharist). Available from the COCU office.

nesses and servants of Christ to the world. But in worship the church does more than just prepare for mission. Worship itself is one of the ways the church engages in its mission until the end of time. Even in places where some forms of mission are forbidden by the state, the faithful assembling of the people for Christian worship is a mighty witness to the gospel. What happens in worship is of vital significance for the world: the church intercedes for the world, and Christ is present for the life of all people. There is no such thing as Christian mission not rooted and renewed continuously in the church's worship. Worship is mission.

41) **Proclamation of the gospel** also is mission. Beyond the gathered worshipping community, faithful telling of the story by which the church lives is an essential part of its apostolate to the world. The church has been entrusted with the story that is life for the world. It is preserved and sent into the world to proclaim that story. The church can never be content simply to signify its faith by deeds done in silence, however essential such deeds are. The church is called as well to confess unambiguously the Christ in whom it lives, and to invite all who will to enter the fellowship of life in Christ through the church, and thus be faithful to its evangelistic task. Proclamation is mission.

42) **Action which embodies Christ's mission** of justice, peace and love is the church's mission, too. Without such action, the church's worship and proclamation are betrayed, "for the tree is known by its fruit."[36] This action is described in many ways in Scripture: it is relief for the poor, release for prisoners, sight for the blind, liberty for the oppressed;[37] it is food for the hungry, drink for those who thirst, welcome for strangers, clothes for those who have none, companionship for those who are sick, imprisoned, or alone.[38] God in Christ has a special concern for those whom the world mistreats or overlooks: the poor, the weak, the oppressed, those excluded from full participation in society, and those who by reason of physical or mental disability, race, language or culture (such as African American, Asian, Pacific Islander, Hispanic, Native American) are dehumanized. Faithful participation in Christ's mission of justice, peace and love for all people, and the integrity of creation, requires repentance of the church: a deliberate turning away from all the various expressions of unconscious racism — individual, corporate, systemic — naming them and renouncing them. But such repentance is not enough unless it results in actions for justice, focused on eliminating those conditions which permit racism to fester and violate human life.

---

[36]Matthew 12:33.

[37]Luke 4:18

[38]Matthew 25:35-40.

43) It is appropriate to add something more specific regarding the church's action in mission, in view of the racial and ethnic diversity of this covenant communion. [39] Christian unity, for churches of predominantly African American membership, is a subject never far removed from struggles to overcome poverty and to achieve social, economic, and racial justice. The struggle for civil rights in this country was rooted in the African American churches, and it became the greatest contribution of these churches to Christian unity in this century. With its holistic concern for the civic, spiritual and material wellbeing of every person, this evangelical movement for human rights gave new meaning to the word from which "ecumenical" is derived, *oikoumene*: "the whole inhabited earth." It embodied "ecumenical altruism": love that leaps all boundaries out of a profound respect for all people. This movement has taught us that where there is no condemnation of idolatry and no call to social justice, there can be no positive or prophetic ecumenical vision of unity or of peace. The covenant communion upon which we enter deliberately claims and shall seek by God's grace to embody this understanding of what it means to be the body of Christ in mission to the world.

44) The Consultation desires that its unity in mission find expression in all three of these dimensions of mission. For the sake of the world, these churches wish to find occasions for worshipping together in covenant communion, and celebrating the eucharist together. For the sake of the world, they seek ways in which their proclamation of the gospel may be made with one voice in covenant communion. For the sake of the world, they seek opportunities for acting together in the service of God's justice, peace and love in the world, that the unity and diversity of this covenant communion may be a sign to all people of God's redemptive will "to unite all things in Christ, things in heaven and things on earth."[40]

Formation of Covenanting Councils

45) Wherever covenanting occurs — nationally, regionally, or locally — one of the inaugural covenanting acts will be the formation of a covenanting council in each such "place." The reason for doing this is that church unity will be neither visible nor organic if it is not embodied in tangible form. The church exists not alone in the mind. It takes up space on the earth. It can be seen. It can act, and be

---

[39]Three of the nine churches in the Consultation on Church Union are composed predominantly of African American membership. A fourth is approximately half black and half white in its composition. The remaining five churches, while having a predominantly Caucasian membership, are racially and ethnically diverse in significant measure.

[40]Ephesians 1:10.

accountable for its actions. In a covenant communion of churches, therefore, it is essential that there be a company of persons who representatively give expression and leadership to its common life. Such groups we refer to as covenanting councils.

46) The primary purpose of these covenanting councils will be to enable the communion of churches in covenant. Several of their functions are of a distinctly ecclesial nature. By giving visible expression to the unity of the churches in covenant communion, the covenanting councils create the corporate ecclesial setting for the ordering of the covenanting ministries of bishops, presbyters, deacons, and lay persons. Among the functions of covenanting councils are:

— ordering the sacrament of Holy Communion in ways that are faithful to the Tradition as claimed in the covenanting agreements, and assembling the people from time to time to celebrate it as one;

— enabling joint ordinations among all the covenanting churches in which reconciled bishops lay on hands with prayer together with the presence and participation of representative ordained and lay persons from as many of the covenanting churches as possible;[41]

— giving joint spiritual oversight (*episkopé*) of the things which enable covenant communion among the churches, including

  – pursuit of inclusiveness,

  – pursuit of a fuller embodiment within each church of the full vision of ministry described in Chapter VII of *The COCU Consensus*,

  – provision of public occasions which visibly bear witness to unity in Christ, such as common baptisms, confirmations, ordinations, and other sacred occasions;

— acting as one in the service of justice on behalf of all for whom justice is delayed or denied, doing so within existing ecumenical bodies where appropriate; and,

— providing opportunity for shared decision-making in our common engagement in Christ's mission in the world.

The covenanting councils may also be given other tasks which the participating churches find appropriate to give them. Covenanting councils will not have authority over the churches. They will derive their authority to act from the judicatories which brought them into being. They will exercise a shared oversight of the covenanting process upon which the churches will enter.

47) This list of functions makes clear that the primary focus of the covenanting process is the local worshiping community, gathered around the Word and sacraments, and giving expression to the church's missionary vocation in the world. It is the local covenanting council,

---

[41]See pp. 23-24, par. 27; see also middle of p. 52.

more than the regional or the national, on which primary attention falls in the covenanting process.

48) **Local covenanting councils** will exist to enable congregations of the covenanting churches, located in close proximity to one another (in the same town or in an urban or rural neighborhood) to live and act as one covenant communion in that place, even while maintaining their distinct existences and traditions. Through a shared life of Word and sacrament, publicly confessing the one faith together, and served by ordained ministers who are fully reconciled and hence fully accessible to all, these congregations will be able to reach out in mission as one people of Christ in ways not possible before they entered into covenant communion.

49) **Regional covenanting councils** bring together representatively those judicatories of the covenanting churches where ordination and oversight is located.[42] They are a collegial expression of shared oversight of the covenanting commitment of the churches, particularly in relation to the ordained ministries, congregations of the faithful, and common mission. Additionally, they facilitate formation of local covenanting councils, and encourage and assist those which have been formed.

50) **The national covenanting council** will encourage regional judicatories to enter into covenanting, and will assist those that have been formed. It will invite other communions of Christ's church to enter the covenant. The national covenanting council will provide a forum where churchwide concerns may be considered, including concerns that arise from local and regional covenanting experience. It will enable the churches to think together about matters of worship, including mutually acceptable liturgical norms for shared worship. It will enable churches to think together about matters of ecclesiastical polity as each church seeks increasingly to embody the vision of ministry contained in *The COCU Consensus*, in partnership with the other covenanting churches. Any necessary amendments to the two documents embodying the basic agreements of the covenant communion shall be recommended to the participating churches by the national covenanting council. In sum, it will give collegial guidance to the covenanting process in matters of a general nature.

51) The covenanting churches will continue to participate fully in the life of other ecumenical bodies. The relationships nurtured through the conciliar movement have done much to bring the covenanting churches into closer relation with each other, and it is anticipated

---

[42]This refers to the ordination of ministers of Word and sacrament (presbyters) and ministers of *episkopé* (bishops). In all of the COCU churches, these are ordained at the middle judicatory level (see footnote 25 on page 23). It is recognized, however, that in some of the member churches there are other ministries in which ordination occurs at the level of the local congregation.

that the ecclesial depth of relationship among the covenanting churches
will mean much to the conciliar movement as well. Councils of churches
represent a broader constituency than do the covenanting councils;
hence, councils of churches will continue to be of great importance to
the covenanting churches. It is intended that the relationship between
covenanting councils and the councils of churches will be a cooperative,
complementary, and mutually enriching one. It is intended that the
funding and human resources now committed by the churches in their
present separateness will not be eroded when they enter into covenant
communion. Covenanting councils are not a substitute for councils of
churches; rather, they give expression to a covenantal form of church
union.

52) Each covenanting council may be organized in such manner
as seems appropriate to the consenting covenanting churches in that
"place," provided only that the following basic agreements be observed:
— covenanting councils shall be composed of elected representatives
   of churches which have formally entered into covenanting through
   affirmative action on *The COCU Consensus* and *Churches in Covenant Communion,* and through participation in the inaugurating
   liturgies of covenanting;
— covenanting councils shall be composed in such a way as to be
   representative of the total ministry of the people of God, lay ministries as well as ordained ministries, within these churches; the
   churches, with appropriate consultation, will determine in what
   way their existing ministries will be represented in the councils,
   and the particular persons who will be sent to them;
— covenanting councils shall be composed in such a way as to be
   inclusive of the diversity which God has given to the churches
   which form them.[43]
The size, organization, and frequency of meeting of the several covenanting councils, as well as their geographical territories or boundaries, shall be determined in the joint discretion of the ecclesiastical
bodies which form them in each "place."[44]

---

[43]*The COCU Consensus*, p. 8, par. 13; pp. 9-10, par. 16-17; and p. 14, par. 6(g).

[44]An illustration of how the covenanting churches in any "place" might wish to organize
their Covenanting Council is described in an Appendix, attached hereto for information on pages
39-40.

V

The Process Of Covenanting

1) The process of covenanting is intended to be implemented by the churches through a series of deliberate steps and stages.

Claiming the Theological Consensus

2) The first formal act of covenanting is for each church to claim *The COCU Consensus: In Quest of a Church of Christ Uniting* (1984). What that means specifically is stated in the Foreword to that document, namely that each participating church is asked, by formal action, to recognize in it:

    [1] an expression, in the matters with which it deals, of the Apostolic faith, order, worship, and witness of the Church,

    [2] an anticipation of the Church Uniting which the participating bodies, by the power of the Holy Spirit, wish to become, and

    [3] a sufficient theological basis for the covenanting acts and the uniting process proposed at this time by the Consultation.[45]

The churches' action on these resolutions began in 1986. It is expected that by 1989 all of the member churches of the Consultation will have had opportunity to consider and act upon them.

Approving the Covenanting Proposal

3) The second formal act of covenanting is for the participating churches to receive, study, and take formal action upon the document, *Churches in Covenant Communion: The Church of Christ Uniting* (1988). What that means specifically is stated in the resolution of transmittal of this document to the churches, issued by the 1988 Plenary of the Consultation on Church Union (see Preface). This document contains the essentials of the covenanting agreements, together with the liturgies by which the covenant is to be inaugurated.

---

[45]*The COCU Consensus*, p. 2.

The Consultation Considers Next Steps

4) After the participating churches have considered and acted upon the proposals of the Consultation contained in the two documents, *The COCU Consensus* and *Churches in Covenant Communion*, the Consultation on Church Union will carefully examine the actions of the churches on these recommendations, and determine next steps accordingly. No judgment has been made in advance regarding the number of churches that must approve the proposals in order for them to be implemented, nor on other questions concerning the nature of the churches' actions upon them. Such matters will be addressed together by the churches, through the Consultation on Church Union, after the participating churches have acted upon the proposals now before them. If the decision of the Consultation is that the actions of the churches justify implementation of the covenanting proposals as presented, the following two sections of this chapter on "The Process of Covenanting" then apply. If the decision is other than that, the Consultation on Church Union in plenary session will itself determine what action to recommend to the churches.

Preparations to Implement Covenanting

5) The fourth step in the covenanting process may be somewhat different for each church. It has to do with the particular preparations that each church will need to make in order to participate fully in the inaugurating liturgies of covenanting. Each church which takes affirmative action on the first two steps described above will then need to take other steps as promptly as possible, internal to its own polity, to prepare itself in whatever ways it may deem to be necessary for the acts of recognition and of reconciliation which are described in the covenanting document and its accompanying liturgies. Specifically this could mean as many as four things:

(a) discovering what categories of ordained ministry within one's polity correspond most closely to that of "bishop," "presbyter," and "deacon" as described in the two documents named above;

(b) making such amendment of one's polity or ecclesiastical system as may be necessary — in good faith, in dialogue with other participating churches, and in the spirit of this covenantal commitment — in order:

     [1] to make possible the participation of one's church in a covenantal form of church union as here proposed,

     [2] to delegate to covenanting councils (upon their formation) sufficient authority to act in the ways described in this document, and

[3] to make possible, through whatever changes may need to be made, full participation within the covenant communion of those who are to be put forward for reconciliation as covenanting bishops and presbyters — utilizing the collegial processes of the Consultation on Church Union to assure mutual acceptability of these forms of ministry within the covenant communion of churches;

(c) naming its representatives to the national service of covenanting, and its representatives to the national covenanting council which will be inaugurated soon thereafter; and

(d) encouraging its regional bodies to name their representatives for participation in regional services of covenanting.

Participation in the Covenanting Liturgies

6) The fifth step in the covenanting process is the act of consummating the new relationship of covenant communion among the churches. Each church will participate representatively in the liturgies of covenanting, by which covenant will be declared, ministries reconciled, covenanting councils inaugurated, and the Eucharist shared by all. The full text of these three liturgies is attached.[46] These covenanting acts are parts of a single reality. Though they occur in three liturgical settings, each is integrally related to the others. These three liturgical actions are described as follows.

7) *The first will be the national service of declaring covenant.* This liturgy will include an act of mutual recognition of each other as churches, together with an act for the reconciliation of a small but representative number of ordained ministers (a bishop, a presbyter, and a deacon) from each church. The primary services for the reconciliation of ordained ministries will be held later, in many regional and local settings: bishops will ordinarily be reconciled in regional liturgies, presbyters and deacons in local liturgies. The national liturgy, however, is chiefly focused upon the formal declaring of the covenant on behalf of the participating churches as a whole. Nonetheless, in so doing, it will anticipate as well the reconciliation of ministries which is to follow both there and elsewhere. The national service will not include an act for the inauguration of a national covenanting council, but will instead express the commitment of the churches to do so later after recognition and reconciliation of ministry has occurred in several regions. The liturgy for declaring covenant among the churches will conclude with the celebration of the Lord's Supper, done in a manner that expresses the new relationship among the participating churches, under the leadership of a reconciled covenanting bishop.

---

[46]See pp. 41ff.

8) *The second liturgical action will be the regional service for the reconciliation of bishops.* This action is intimately related to the first. Therefore, the first of these regional services will occur in close conjunction with the national service. The choice of location for the national service will be in part made in light of the readiness of the middle judicatories of the covenanting churches in that place to enter promptly into the implementation of the covenant through the reconciliation of their ordained ministers of regional *episkopé*. It is hoped that several of these regional services will be held immediately following the national service, perhaps simultaneously with one another at different places across the country. The reconciliation of bishops will be accomplished through the mutual recognition of one another's ministry of *episkopé* and through a mutual laying on of hands among the bishops, together with other appropriate signs, and prayer. The regional service will include an act for the inaugurating of a regional covenanting council. The regional service will conclude with the celebration of the Holy Communion, done in a way that expresses the new relationship among the participating churches.

9) *The third liturgical action will be the local service for celebrating the covenant, for reconciling presbyters, and for welcoming deacons and other ordained ministers of governance.* These local services will occur within regions where there has already been a regional service for the reconciliation of bishops. They will of course occur in many localities throughout the region. The first such local celebration may well occur on the same day as the regional service of reconciliation of bishops, and possibly in the same place. The local service will include an acknowledgment of the reconciliation of bishops that has occurred in that region. It will then move to the reconciliation of presbyters, this being essential to eucharistic fellowship. To that end, the liturgy will include the laying on of the hands of a reconciled bishop upon each of the presbyters there gathered, together with the giving of the hand of fellowship and other appropriate signs of welcome.

10) The diaconal ministries of the churches are now so dissimilar to one another that a meaningful act of reconciliation into a single ministry of deacon is difficult to contemplate at this time. Nonetheless, every church does engage in diaconal ministry; some of these diaconal ministers are ordained and others are unordained. So also, each church provides in some manner for the participation of other persons in ecclesial governance — persons variously defined as Elders, members of the Vestry or of the Official Board. For some, these ministries of governance are an ordained office, and for others they are not. Hence, no meaningful act of reconciliation into a single ministry of governance can be effected at this time. Nonetheless, the local liturgy will include a public act for the mutual welcoming of all ordained deacons and all

ordained ministers of governance within the shared life of the covenant communion of churches, but it will not include a liturgical act for the reconciliation of these varied ministries.

11) The service will include an act for the inauguration of a local covenanting council, and will be concluded with the celebration of the Eucharist, done in a way that expresses the new relationship among the participating churches.

The Expanding Process of Covenanting

12) It is not anticipated that covenanting will commence in all places at the same time. While the national church bodies will declare covenant and will proceed sometime thereafter to form a national covenanting council, regional church judicatories will in turn celebrate covenant, reconcile ministries, and form a regional covenanting council when they are ready to do so. Even after the regional judicatories of the churches have entered into covenanting, groups of congregations within the region will celebrate the covenant and form a local covenanting council when they are prepared so to do. Relationships can be encouraged but not compelled.

13) For an indefinite period, therefore, there may be some unevenness and indeed some anomaly in this covenant communion of churches. One may judge, however, that the anomaly will not be greater than the divisions which now fracture the one body and the one Table of Christ. Covenanting provides a means whereby the Holy Spirit may draw the churches into an ever widening and deepening unity, where and when the Spirit wills.

Appendix

The Reason For An Appendix

1) The matters dealt with in this appendix are not a part of the covenanting agreements. They are suggestions offered to those who will bear responsibility for the organization of covenanting councils in each place. Locating these suggestions in an appendix rather than among the covenanting agreements themselves reflects the understanding that, while such councils are indeed an element of covenanting, their precise structural form is not. The organizational arrangement of these bodies is seen as a matter of local judgment which may well vary from time to time and from place to place.

Composition of Covenanting Councils

2) It is suggested that the covenanting councils be composed of representatives of each of the reconciled and welcomed ordained ministries (in such numbers, in such proportions among the ministries, and for such terms of service as the covenanting bodies shall themselves jointly decide in each place) together with representative lay members of the covenanting churches, in number at least equal to the sum of the representative ordained ministers.[47] In local covenanting councils, it may be considered permissible for bishops to be represented by deputies either from their own or from another covenanting communion. Since the covenanting council is to be a model of inclusiveness for all the covenanting churches, the composition of each communion's representation in the council should be negotiated in advance, so that the council will reflect the diversity of the church's membership.[48]

Accountability of Covenanting Councils

3) It is suggested that the accountability of the covenanting councils be regarded as a collective accountability to the bodies which brought them into being: the national covenanting council to the national governing bodies of the covenanting churches, the regional covenanting

---

[47]*The COCU Consensus*, pp. 43-44, par. 25; also p. 45, par. 26(f).

[48]*The COCU Consensus*, p. 8, par. 13; pp. 9-10, par. 16-17; and p. 14, par. 6(g).

councils to the ecclesiastical middle judicatories which formed them, and the local covenanting council to the worshipping congregations of the covenanting churches which entered into covenant communion located in that place. The relationship between different levels of covenanting councils — local, regional, or national — is suggested to be one of mutual caring and encouragement, but not of power, as they together seek to further the integrity of the covenant communion of churches, of which they are the most tangible embodiment.

Administration of Covenanting Councils

4) Administrative structures are not an inherent aspect of these proposals at any level: local, regional, or national. The covenanting churches in any place or at any level may choose to organize themselves as they deem appropriate and to provide for themselves such administrative help as they may need, if any. The churches themselves — locally, regionally, or nationally — will know when or whether they need any administrative assistance in pursuing their covenant communion, and such matters are left entirely in their discretion.

Worship in Covenanting Councils

5) In light of the essentially ecclesial nature of the covenanting councils, it is suggested that their meetings be regularly marked by corporate acts of worship, including from time to time the celebration of the Eucharist. Through the Consultation on Church Union, the churches have developed many resources for such common worship, among which may be mentioned the COCU Liturgy for the Lord's Supper (approved by all the participating churches), *Guidelines for Interim Eucharistic Fellowship*, the COCU lectionary of agreed texts (now serving a much larger consistency in a modified form), and the COCU Lenten Booklet of devotional readings.

PART II

Liturgies
for Inauguration of Covenanting

A National Service

For Declaring Covenant, Reconciling Ordained Ministers, And Celebrating The Sacrament of The Lord's Supper

OUTLINE OF THE SERVICE

INTRODUCTORY AND PENITENTIAL RITES
>Acclamation
>Declaration of Purpose
>Prayer of Confession
>Declaration of Forgiveness

LITURGY OF THE WORD
>Prayer for Illumination
>First Reading – Old Testament
>Psalm
>Second Reading – New Testament
>Hymn
>Gospel
>Sermon
>Nicene Creed

DECLARING THE COVENANT
>Introduction
>Covenant Statements
>Covenant
>Peace

PRAYERS OF THE PEOPLE

**RECONCILING MINISTERS WITH
ORDAINING RESPONSIBILITIES**
>Processional Hymn
>Presentation
>Declaration of Intention
>Renewal of Vows
>Laying on of Hands
>Prayer for the Wider Exercise of Ministry

**RECONCILING PRESBYTERAL
MINISTERS OF WORD AND SACRAMENT**
>Presentation
>Renewal of Vows
>Prayer for the Wider Exercise of Ministry
>Signs of Reconciliation

**WELCOMING ORDAINED DEACONS AND
ORDAINED MINISTERS OF GOVERNANCE**
Presentation
Declaration of Intention
Renewal of Vows
Prayer for the Wider Exercise of Ministry
Signs of Welcome

SERVICE OF THE TABLE
Offering
Preparing the Table of the Lord

A National Service

**For Declaring Covenant, Reconciling Ordained Ministers,
And Celebrating The Sacrament of The Lord's Supper**

INTRODUCTORY AND PENITENTIAL RITES

Acclamation

A leader of worship says:

> Blessed be our God.

People: **For ever and ever.   Amen.**

Declaration of Purpose

The leader then makes a declaration of purpose:

> We are gathered here as representatives of the churches
> we now name:
>
> . . . .
> . . . .
> . . . .
>
> Our purpose is to declare the unity of our faith, confess
> the brokenness of our common life, renew the covenant
> of grace by which we are bound to God and to each
> other, and seal this new experience of oneness by shar-
> ing together the Supper of our Lord. Already we have
> recognized each other's baptism into Christ's body.
> By the covenant which we now declare we enter into
> a new and visible form of unity among the churches
> which, though being many, are one body in Christ.

Prayer of Confession

A leader of worship announces the prayer of confession:

> Let us confess our sins to God who is faithful and just,
> through the saving power of the life, death, and resur-
>   rection of Jesus Christ,
> forgives our sins and cleanses us from all unrighteous-
>   ness.

47

People: **Ever-living God,**
                our Judge and Healer,
                have mercy upon us.

Leader: We profess to love you with heart, mind, soul and
                    strength,
                and to love our neighbors as we love our selves.
                Yet by the sinfulness of our division
                we transgress your commandments
                and violate your perfect will.

People: **Ever-loving God,**
                our Guide and Liberator,
                have mercy on us.

Leader: We now confess to you and to one another
                that we have been unwilling to live together in com-
                    munion.
                We acknowledge that our division
                has obscured our witness to the Christian faith,
                diminished the fullness of our worship,
                hindered the exercise of ministry,
                and limited the mission of justice and love
                in all the world.

People: **Ever-forgiving God,**
                Source of Compassion and Righteousness,
                have mercy upon us.

Leader: Forgive us our offenses and help us amend what we are.
                Deliver us from personal and institutional violence
                toward one another and toward all powerless people
                    everywhere.
                By the example of Jesus,
                help us to obey your commandments,
                edify your people, and proclaim your glory.

People: **Ever-living God,**
                Loving and Sustaining Presence,
                have mercy upon us.

Declaration of Forgiveness

Leader: The ever-faithful God,
                whose tender mercies are revealed through
                Jesus Christ,

> forgives us all our sins,
> and by the gifts of the Holy Spirit,
> empowers us to live with faith, joy and love.

People: **Thanks be to God.**

A hymn of praise is sung.

LITURGY OF THE WORD

Prayer for Illumination

A leader of worship offers a prayer for illumination:

> Blessed God,
> who caused all holy Scriptures to be written for our
>   learning:
> Grant us so to hear them,
> read, mark, learn, and inwardly digest them,
> that we may embrace and ever hold fast
> the blessed hope of everlasting life,
> which you have given us in our
>   Savior Jesus Christ;
> who lives and reigns with you and
>   the Holy Spirit,
> one God, for ever and ever.

People: **Amen.**

First Reading – Old Testament

Reader: A reading from (name of the book).

After the reading the reader says:

> The Word of God.

People: **Thanks be to God.**

Psalm

A psalm is sung. A period of silence may follow.

Second Reading – New Testament

Reader: A reading from (name of the book).

After the reading the reader says:

> The Word of God.

People: **Thanks be to God.**

Hymn

A hymn, psalm, or spiritual song is sung.

Gospel

The Holy Scriptures are brought to the appointed place for the reading of the gospel.

Reader: The holy gospel of Jesus Christ according to
                   (name of the book).

People: **Glory to you, O Christ.**

After the gospel, the reader says:

                   The gospel of Christ.

People: **Praise to you, O Christ.**

The Sermon

Nicene Creed

A leader invites the people to join in proclaiming the Church's faith, as expressed in the Nicene Creed.

People: **We believe in one God,**
                   the Father, the Almighty,
                   maker of heaven and earth,
                   of all that is, seen and unseen.

                   We believe in one Lord, Jesus Christ,
                   the only Son of God,
                   eternally begotten of the Father,
                   God from God, Light from Light,
                   true God from true God,
                   begotten, not made,
                   of one Being with the Father;
                   through him all things were made.
                   For us and for our salvation
                      he came down from heaven,
                      was incarnate of the Holy Spirit and
                         the Virgin Mary
                      and became truly human.
                   For our sake he was crucified under
                      Pontius Pilate;
                   he suffered death and was buried.

On the third day he rose again
in accordance with the Scriptures;
he ascended into heaven
and is seated at the right hand of the Father.
He will come again in glory to judge the
living and the dead,
and his kingdom will have no end.

We believe in the Holy Spirit, the Lord,
the giver of life,
who proceeds from the Father and the Son,
who with the Father and the Son is worshiped
and glorified,
who has spoken through the prophets.
We believe in one holy catholic and
apostolic Church.
We acknowledge one baptism for the
forgiveness of sins.
We look for the resurrection of the dead,
and the life of the world to come. Amen.

A hymn, psalm, or spiritual song is sung.

DECLARING THE COVENANT

Introduction

A leader says: Moved by the Spirit of God, we enter into this covenant
with one another.

Covenant Statements

*Representatives of the churches, from the midst of the people, proclaim
the following covenant statements:*

A representative:

We covenant to receive into our churches, without
impediment, Christians baptized in all churches bound
by this covenant; and to baptize in ways that are faithful
to the one baptism affirmed by the churches.

All sing: **By God's grace, this is our covenant.**

A representative:

We covenant to struggle against bias and prejudice

which leads to injustice against all people and to seek a unity with wholeness where differences are affirmed, accepted and celebrated as gifts of God for the common good.

All sing: **By God's grace, this is our covenant.**

A representative:

We have covenanted to renew our separate churches according to the CONSENSUS of the Consultation on Church Union that they may be truly catholic, truly evangelical, and truly reformed.

All sing: **By God's grace, this is our covenant.**

A representative:

We covenant to recognize and affirm the ordained ministries of each covenanting church here gathered, acknowledging that each partakes of the one ministry of Christ; and we henceforth will incorporate women and men into these ministries by services of ordination ordered so as to include the presence and participation of representatives from the covenanting churches.

All sing: **By God's grace, this is our covenant.**

A representative:

We covenant to break bread in remembrance of Christ: in our congregations to welcome one another to commune in the eucharistic meal, and to meet frequently as covenanting churches and congregations for eucharistic fellowship, and on all such occasions to be faithful to our claimed tradition.

All sing: **By God's grace, this is our covenant.**

A representative:

We covenant to act together in the ways we make decisions and order our work; and we give ourselves anew to God's mission: to preach good news to the poor, to proclaim release to the captive and recovery of sight to the blind, and to set at liberty those who are oppressed, and to proclaim the acceptable year of the Lord.

All sing: **By God's grace, this is our covenant.**

A representative:
> We covenant to continue a life of penitence and renewal, to establish and participate in Covenanting Councils on national, regional, and local levels, and to invite other churches to enter into this covenanted life.

All sing: **By God's grace, this is our covenant.**

A leader says: By our covenant, our churches now recognize each other as true Churches of Jesus Christ, and as authentic expressions of the one, holy, catholic, and apostolic Church. We therefore affirm:

> Faith in the one God who through the Word and in the Spirit creates, redeems, and sanctifies.

All sing: **Amen.**

A leader says: We affirm:
> Commitment to Jesus Christ as Savior and Lord.

All sing: **Amen.**

A leader says: We affirm:
> Obedience to the Holy Scriptures which testify to Tradition and to which Tradition testifies, as containing those things necessary for salvation as well as being the rule and ultimate standard of faith.

All sing: **Amen.**

A leader says: We affirm:
> Faithful participation in the two sacraments ordained by Christ: baptism and holy Communion.

All sing: **Amen.**

A leader says: We affirm:
> Commitment to the evangelical and prophetic mission of God and to the service of God's reign of justice and peace.

All sing: **Amen.**

A leader says: We affirm:
> Recognition that the lay and ordained ministries of each church are apostolic, manifest gifts, and partake of the one ministry of Christ.

All sing: **Amen.**

Covenant

*The representatives of each church in turn make the following decla-
ration in unison:*

> In the peace of Christ,
> we who represent _____
> give ourselves to you by this covenant of unity,
> and we recognize you as members with us
> in Christ's body, the Church.
> We pray that God will draw our churches together,
> and knit us into one people
> so that the world may believe.

*A hymn of commitment is sung, such as Charles Wesley's Covenant
Hymn ("Come, Let Us Use the Grace Divine") or some other suitable
hymn.*

A leader then prays:

> God of peace and reconciliation,
> by your Holy Spirit free us to greet one another
> in the peace that only you can give.
> Grant this through Christ our Lord.

All sing: **Amen, Amen, Amen.**

Peace

A leader says: The peace of Christ be with you.

All respond: **And also with you.**

*The representatives of the churches and all present exchange the peace
with appropriate words and gestures.*

PRAYERS OF THE PEOPLE

*After all have exchanged the peace, the following prayer of intercession
may then be offered.*

Leader: Holy Trinity, One God,
                let your glory fill the world.

People: **All praise to you, God our Creator,**
                for by your Word and Spirit
                you created the heavens and the earth,
                filled them with life,

and declared everything good.

All praise to you, God our Redeemer,
for sending apostles, prophets, teachers,
    and martyrs,
inspired by your Spirit
to speak the word of life;
but especially for becoming fully human
    in Jesus Christ.

All praise to you, God our Helper,
as wisdom you inspire us to do the truth,
as power you strengthen us to do justice.

Holy God, let your glory fill the world.

Leader: Sovereign God, hear our prayer
            for the heavens and the earth,
            created in beauty
            but now languishing in sin.

People: **Stir up in us passion for the earth**
                and its care.
            Inspire us and all the peoples of the world
            to respect and enjoy creation as you intend.

Leader: Merciful God, we pray for the human family
                everywhere
            and especially those who suffer
            from poverty and oppression.

People: **Shape us and all other churches**
            that we may continue the work of
                Jesus Christ,
            preaching good news and deliverance
            and working for the coming of your
                rule on earth.

Leader: God of justice, hear our prayer
            for our churches.
            Make us to be a conscience to this nation.

People: **Make us witnesses to the vision**
            of a society that is just and responsible.
            Enable us to be healers of people
                and institutions,
            wounded in the struggle to live faithfully.
            Help us express the gospel in daily life
            until all creation proclaims your glory.

Leader: O God, Creator of heaven and earth,
                   Redeemer of the world,
                   Sanctifier of the faithful:

People: **Have mercy upon us**
                   and grant us your peace.
                   Holy, blessed, and glorious Trinity, One God,
                   let your glory fill the world.
                   To you be all praise and thanksgiving,
                   now and forever more.
                   Amen.

*Here, after a Hymn and Benediction, a recess for a meal may be taken,
or there may be a musical offering such as a* Te Deum.

RECONCILING MINISTERS WITH
ORDAINING RESPONSIBILITIES

Processional Hymn

After all assemble again for worship, a hymn is sung during the procession of those who will preside and the ministers to be reconciled.

Presentation

*Each covenanting church presents a person whom it has named for
the exercise of ordaining responsibility, that these ministers may be
reconciled to one another. Representatives of the churches who present
these ministers say to the leaders of the service:*

All Representatives:
                   We bring before you these persons
                   who are to be received by all
                   as bishops in the Church of God.
                   They have confessed the Christian faith
                      and have been baptized.
                   They have heard God's call
                   and have been ordained by their churches
                   to the ministry of word, sacrament, and order.
                   In their own churches they have exercised
                   a ministry of apostolic oversight.

Declaration of Intention

Leader: It is our intention, within this covenant which we have made with each other, that each of these bishops, now being reconciled by a mutual laying on of hands and prayer, will recognize and receive the ministry and tradition of the others. Our purpose is that these ministers become reconciled, that they may henceforth serve together as representative pastoral ministers of oversight, unity, and continuity in the Church, fulfilling the ministry of bishop as expressed in the theological consensus affirmed by our churches.

Renewal of Vows

The presiding minister addresses these persons with questions to which they and the congregation make their response:

Leader: Will you, in the power of the Spirit, continue the life of Christian discipleship which began when you were baptized?

Answer: I will, by God's help.

People: **Amen, Alleluia!**

Leader: Will you continue to be faithful to the ministry which you have received?

Answer: I will, by God's help.

People: **Amen, Alleluia!**

Leader: Do you affirm the covenant of unity which our churches are making with each other?

Answer: I do, by God's help.

People: **Amen, Alleluia!**

Leader: Will you commit yourself to the responsibilities of the office of bishop according to the principles set forth in the covenant our churches have made with one another?

Answer: I will, by God's help.

People: **Amen, Alleluia!**

Leader: Will you be obedient to God, faithful to the gospel of Christ, responsible to the Church, and zealous in your work as minister and bishop?

Answer: I will, for the sake of Jesus Christ.

People: **Amen, Alleluia!**

Laying on of Hands

The covenanting bishops lay hands upon one another in silence.

Prayer for the Wider Exercise of Ministry

When all have received this sign of reconciliation, the covenanting bishops offer this prayer:

> We give you thanks, O God,
> for calling us into this new covenant.
> Complete in us your gifts,
> received and exercised in our separation,
> that we may now minister together as bishops
>   in your church.
>
> Give us grace to manifest
> and set forth the unity of your church,
> proclaim the Christian faith,
> maintain worship in spirit and in truth,
> feed the flock of Christ,
> and in all things care for your church.
>
> All this we ask through Jesus Christ,
> who lives with you and the Holy Spirit,
> one God, now and for ever.

People: **Amen.**

A psalm, hymn, or spiritual song is sung.

RECONCILING PRESBYTERAL MINISTERS
OF WORD AND SACRAMENT

Presentation

Each covenanting church presents a person whom it has named for the presbyteral ministry of Word and sacrament, that these ministers may be reconciled to one another. Representatives of the participating churches address the bishops:

All Representatives:

> We bring before you these ordained presbyters
> who minister within the life and discipline
>   of our respective churches.

> They have studied the Word of God and the
>   faith of the church
> and have prepared themselves for public
>   service in the church
> in the name of Christ.
> They have been examined and ordained by
>   the laying on of hands and prayer.
> They are now called to enter more fully
> into the covenanting and reconciling
>   communion
> that is being created among us by the Spirit
>   of God.

Renewal of Vows

Bishop: As Presbyters you have been ordained to serve among the baptized members of the people of God as ministers of Word and sacrament. In this role you bear responsibility for the discipline of the church and are teachers and preachers of the faith, so that the world may believe and the church be renewed, equipped, and strengthened in its ministry.

Do you here, in the presence of Christ and this congregation, renew your commitment to this ministry which your have received?

Answer: I do, with God's help.

Bishop: Will you then continue the life of Christian discipleship which began when you were baptized?

Answer: I will, by God's help.

Bishop: Do you affirm the covenant of unity which our churches are making with one another?

Answer: I do, by God's help.

Bishop: Do you renew your commitment to proclaim the Word of God and administer the sacraments of the New Covenant?

Answer: I do, by God's help.

Bishop: Will you be a faithful and zealous pastor and servant of those committed to your care in the name of Jesus Christ, the Good Shepherd?

Answer: I will, by God's help.

Prayer for the Wider Exercise of Ministry

All Covenanting Presbyters:

> We give you thanks, O God,
> for calling us into this new covenant.
> Complete in us your gifts,
> received and exercised in our separation,
> that we may now minister together as
>   presbyters in your church.
>
> Give us grace to preach your word
>   with boldness,
> administer your sacraments with faith,
> and care for your church in unity and love,
> to the glory of your Name.
>
> All this we ask through Jesus Christ,
> who lives with you and the Holy Spirit,
> one God, now and for ever.

People: **Amen.**

A hymn invoking the Holy Spirit is sung.

Signs of Reconciliation

During the singing of this hymn, stations are formed, each consisting of a bishop and a lay person. Each presbyter goes to one of these stations to receive, first from the bishop and then from the lay person, the signs of reconciliation for wider ministry. The sign of reconciliation given by the bishop is the placing of the hand of blessing upon the head in silence. The sign of reconciliation given by the lay person is the hand of fellowship or the holy kiss.

As the reconciled presbyters return to their places, they greet one another and other members of the assembly in the love, joy, and peace of Christ.

A psalm, hymn, or spiritual song may be sung.

WELCOMING ORDAINED DEACONS AND ORDAINED MINISTERS OF GOVERNANCE

Presentation

Each covenanting church presents a person whom it has named to the ministry of deacon, that these ministers may be welcomed by the

churches. Also, each covenanting church which has an ordained minis-
try of governance brings forward a person whom it has named to that
ministry, that these ministers too may be welcomed by the churches.
Representatives of the churches presenting these ministers say to the
bishops:

All Representatives:
> We bring before you these deacons
> and ordained ministers of governance.
> They have studied the Word of God
> and the faith of the Church
> and have prepared themselves for service in
> > the Church in the name of Christ.
> They have been examined and ordained
> by the laying on of hands and prayer.
> They now present themselves
> because of their desire to enter more fully
> into the covenanting and reconciling
> > communion
> that is here being created by the Spirit
> > of God.

Declaration of Intention

Bishop: All of our churches engage in diaconal ministry; so
              also all of our churches provide for the participation
              of other persons in ecclesiastical governance, ordained
              and unordained. Without presuming to reconcile these
              ordained offices into a single ministry of service and
              governance at this time, we now welcome these or-
              dained ministers within the shared life of the covenant
              communion of our churches, anticipating the day when
              our growth in unity will make possible a full reconcili-
              ation of all these ordained ministers of the church.

Renewal of Vows

Another   You have been ordained to serve your churches in their
Bishop: order and mission in Christ.
              The covenanting churches recognize that your minis-
              tries have been exercised in a variety of ways. We
              now welcome you to your ministry within this covenant
              communion which is now coming into being.

              Do you here, in the presence of Christ and of us as

	representatives of his Church, renew your commitment to the ministry you have received?
Answer:	I do.
Bishop:	Will you continue the life of Christian discipleship which began when you were baptized?
Answer:	I will, by God's help.
Bishop:	Do you affirm the covenant of unity which our churches are making with each other?
Answer:	I do, by God's help.
Bishop:	Will you renew your commitment to help the people of God in their worship, witness, and service?
Answer:	I will, by God's help.

Prayer for the Wider Exercise of Ministry

All Covenanting Deacons and Ordained Ministers of Governance

We give you thanks, O God,
for calling us into this new covenant.
Complete in us your gifts,
received and exercised in our separation,
that we may continue to be servants in
        pastoral care and governance,
and leaders of the church's mission
        in the world.

Give us grace that we may minister together
        in unity and love
that the world may know Jesus Christ.

All this we ask through him,
who lives with you and the Holy Spirit,
one God, now and for ever.

People: Amen.

A hymn invoking the Holy Spirit is sung.

Signs of Welcome

During the singing of this hymn, stations are formed, each consisting of a bishop and a lay person. Each ordained deacon and ordained minister of governance goes to one of these stations to receive, first from the bishop and then from the lay person, the signs of welcome into the wider ministry. The welcoming sign given by the bishop is the placing of the hand of blessing upon the head in silence. The welcoming sign given by the lay person is the hand of fellowship or the holy kiss.

As the welcomed deacons and ministers of governance return to their places, they greet one another and other members of the assembly in the love, joy, and peace of Christ.

A psalm, hymn, or spiritual song is sung.

SERVICE OF THE TABLE

Offering

An Offering is received for the poor and oppressed.

Preparing the Table of the Lord

During the Offertory, newly welcomed deacons and ordained ministers of governance bring to the altar gifts that represent the life and work of their respective churches.The elements for the Eucharist are brought to the Table of the Lord.

The Eucharist is then celebrated using the rite contained in the Sacrament of the Lord's Supper (1984), *beginning with the Great Thanksgiving.*

End of the National Service

A Regional Service

**For Affirming Covenant,
Reconciling Ministers with Ordaining Responsibilities,
Inaugurating Regional Covenanting Councils,
And Celebrating The Sacrament of The Lord's Supper**

OUTLINE OF THE SERVICE

INTRODUCTORY AND PENITENTIAL RITES
Acclamation
Declaration of Purpose
Prayer of Confession
Declaration of Forgiveness

LITURGY OF THE WORD
Prayer for Illumination
First Reading – Old Testament
Psalm
Second Reading – New Testament
Hymn
Gospel
Sermon

AFFIRMING THE COVENANT
Introduction
Thanksgiving
Affirmation of the Covenant
Peace

**RECONCILING MINISTERS WITH
ORDAINING RESPONSIBILITIES**
Presentation
Declaration of Intention
Renewal of Vows
Laying on of Hands
Prayer for the Wider Exercise of Ministry

INAUGURATING A REGIONAL COVENANTING COUNCIL
Presentation
The Charge
Prayer to Affirm the Council
Response of the People
Dismissal of the Covenanting Council

SERVICE OF THE TABLE
Offering
Preparing the Table of the Lord

A Regional Service

For Affirming Covenant,
Reconciling Ministers with Ordaining Responsibilities,
Inaugurating Regional Covenanting Councils,
And Celebrating The Sacrament of The Lord's Supper

INTRODUCTORY AND PENITENTIAL RITES

Festive music may be played. The people of God wait silently upon the Holy Spirit. Representatives of the churches and those designated to lead the service enter in silence.

Acclamation

A leader of worship says:

Blessed be our God.

People: **For ever and ever. Amen.**

Declaration of Purpose

The leader then makes a declaration of purpose:

We are gathered here as representatives of the churches we now name:

· ·
· ·
· ·

Our purpose is to reconcile the ministers who are responsible for ordination. By this act, we continue what began on (date) at (place of National Service) when representatives of our churches declared a covenant with one another. On that day they promised before God to enter into a new relationship of faith, worship, and witness. Today we too confess the sin and scandal of division and affirm the covenant our churches have already begun. We intend to establish a covenanting council that in our region will oversee growth toward unity.

69

Prayer of Confession

A leader of worship announces the prayer of confesssion:

> Let us confess our sins to God who is faithful
> and just,
> through the saving power of the life, death,
> and resurrection of Jesus Christ,
> forgives our sins and cleanses us from
> all unrighteousness.

People: **Ever-living God,**
our Judge and Healer,
have mercy upon us.

Leader: We profess to love you with heart, mind, soul
and strength,
and to love our neighbors as we love ourselves.
Yet by the sinfulness of our division
we transgress your commandments
and violate your perfect will.

People: **Ever-loving God,**
our Guide and Liberator,
have mercy on us.

Leader: We now confess to you and to one another
that we have been unwilling to live together
in communion.
We acknowledge that our division
has obscured our witness to the Christian faith,
diminished the fullness of our worship,
hindered the exercise of ministry,
and limited the mission of justice and love
in all the world.

People: **Ever-forgiving God,**
Source of Compassion and Righteousness,
have mercy upon us.

Leader: Forgive us our offenses and help us amend
what we are.
Deliver us from personal and institutional violence
toward one another and toward all powerless
people everywhere.
By the example of Jesus,
help us to obey your commandments,
edify your people, and proclaim your glory.

People: **Ever-living God,**
                  Loving and Sustaining Presence,
                  have mercy upon us.

Declaration of Forgiveness

Leader: The ever-faithful God,
                  whose tender mercies are revealed through
                       Jesus Christ,
                  forgives us all our sins,
                  and by the gifts of the Holy Spirit,
                  empowers us to live with faith, joy and love.

People: **Thanks be to God.**

A hymn of praise is sung.

LITURGY OF THE WORD

Prayer for Illumination

A leader of worship offers a prayer for illumination:

                  O God,
                  whose Son is the good shepherd of your people:
                  grant that when we hear his voice
                  we may know the one who calls us each by name,
                  and follow where he leads,
                  through the same Jesus Christ our Lord.

People: **Amen.**

First Reading – Old Testament

Reader: A reading from (name of the book).

After the reading the reader says:

                  The Word of God.

People: **Thanks be to God.**

Psalm

A psalm is sung. A period of silence may follow.

Second Reading – New Testament

Reader: A reading from (name of the book).

After the reading the reader says:

> The Word of God.

People: **Thanks be to God.**

Hymn

A hymn, psalm, or spiritual song is sung.

Gospel

The Holy Scriptures are brought to the appointed place for the reading of the gospel.

Reader: The holy gospel of Jesus Christ according to (name of the book).

People: **Glory to you, O Christ.**

After the gospel, the reader says:

> The gospel of Christ.

People: **Praise to you, O Christ.**

The Sermon

After the sermon a hymn, psalm, or spiritual song is sung.

AFFIRMING THE COVENANT

Introduction

Leader: Sisters and brothers in Christ, in a solemn act of prayer our churches, through authorized representatives, made covenant with each other. They testified to the grace of God that we already enjoy despite our separation; and promised to worship and work, from this time forward, in ways that are mutually acceptable. Joyfully we received each other as members together in Christ's Body, the Church, and sealed this act with the peace of Christ and the sacrament of Holy Communion.

Let us now, as authorized represenatatives of our churches in this region, offer our prayers of thanksgiving for this growth toward unity in Christ and own this covenant for ourselves.

Thanksgiving

People: **God of steadfast love,**
you have called us into covenant with you
and each other.
For this new relationship in Christ,
mutual responsibility,
and promise of strengthened witness to the gospel,
we offer you our thanks.
God of steadfast love,
all praise is yours.

Affirmation of the Covenant

Leader: Moved by God we affirm this covenant which our churches have made.

A leader: We covenant to receive into our churches, without impediment, Christians baptized in all churches bound by this covenant; and to baptize in ways that are faithful to the one baptism affirmed by the churches.

All sing: **By God's grace, this is our covenant.**

A leader: We covenant to struggle against bias and prejudice which leads to injustice against all people and to seek a unity with wholeness where differences are affirmed, acccepted and celebrated as gifts of God for the common good.

All sing: **By God's grace, this is our covenant.**

A leader: We have covenanted to renew our separate churches according to the CONSENSUS of the Consultation on Church Union that they may be truly catholic, truly evangelical, and truly reformed.

All sing: **By God's grace, this is our covenant.**

A leader: We covenant to recognize and affirm the ordained ministries of each covenant church here gathered, acknowledging that each partakes of the one ministry of Christ; and we henceforth will incorporate women and men into these ministries by services of ordination ordered so as to include the presence and participation of representatives from the covenanting churches.

All sing: **By God's grace, this is our covenant.**

A leader: We covenant to break bread in remembrance of Christ: in our congregations to welcome one another to commune in the eucharistic meal, and to meet frequently as covenanting churches and congregations for eucharistic fellowship, and on all such occasions to be faithful to our claimed tradition.

All sing: **By God's grace, this is our covenant.**

A leader: We covenant to act together in the ways we make decisions and order our work; and we give ourselves anew to God's mission: to preach good news to the poor, to proclaim release to the captive and recovery of sight to the blind, and to set at liberty those who are oppressed, and to proclaim the acceptable year of the Lord.

All sing: **By God's grace, this is our covenant.**

A leader: We covenant to continue a life of penitence and renewal, to establish and participate in Covenanting Councils on national, regional, and local levels, and to invite other churches to enter into this covenanted life.

All sing: **By God's grace, this is our covenant.**

Peace

Leader: Reconciling God of peace, by your Holy Spirit free us to greet each other in the peace that only Christ can give.

People: **Knit our churches into one people,
so that the world may believe in Christ
whom you sent into the world that all may find life.
Amen.**

After the participating churches have made this declaration, representatives shall exchange the peace, each person taking the hands of others between his/her own hands, or embracing, saying:

The peace of Christ be with you.

After all representatives have both received and given the peace, the entire assembly is then invited to exchange signs and greetings of peace.

A hymn, psalm, or spiritual song is sung.

RECONCILING MINISTERS WITH ORDAINING RESPONSIBILITIES

Presentation

Each covenanting church presents those whom it has named for the exercise of ordaining responsibility, that these ministers may be reconciled to one another. Representatives of the churches who present these ministers say to the leaders of the service:

All Representatives:

We bring before you these persons
who are to be received by all
as bishops in the Church of God.
They have confessed the Christian faith
    and have been baptized.
They have heard God's call
and have been ordained by their churches
to the ministry of word, sacrament,
    and order.
In their own churches they have exercised
    a ministry of apostolic oversight.

Declaration of Intention

Leader:

It is our intention, within this covenant which we have made with each other, that each of these bishops, now being reconciled by a mutual laying on of hands and prayer, will recognize and receive the ministry and tradition of the others. Our purpose is that these ministers become reconciled, that they may henceforth serve together as representative pastoral ministers of oversight, unity, and continuity in the Church, fulfilling the ministry of bishop as expressed in the theological consensus affirmed by our churches.

Renewal of Vows

The presiding minister addresses these persons with questions to which they and the congregation make their response:

Leader:

Will you, in the power of the Spirit,
continue the life of Christian discipleship
which began when you were baptized?

Answer:

I will, by God's help.

People: **Amen, Alleluia!**

Leader: Will you continue to be faithful to the ministry which you have received?

Answer: I will, by God's help.

People: **Amen, Alleluia!**

Leader: Do you affirm the covenant of unity which our churches are making with each other?

Answer: I do, by God's help.

People: **Amen, Alleluia!**

Leader: Will you commit yourself to the responsibilities of the office of bishop according to the principles set forth in the covenant our churches have made with one another?

Answer: I will, by God's help.

People: **Amen, Alleluia!**

Leader: Will you be obedient to God, faithful to the gospel of Christ, responsible to the Church, and zealous in your work as minister and bishop?

Answer: I will, by God's help.

People: **Amen, Alleluia!**

Laying on of Hands

The covenanting bishops lay hands upon one another in silence.

Prayer for the Wider Exercise of Ministry

When all have received this sign of reconciliation, the covenanting bishops offer this prayer:

> We give you thanks, O God,
> for calling us into this new covenant.
> Complete in us your gifts,

> received and exercised in our separation,
> that we may now minister together as bishops
> in your church.
>
> Give us grace to manifest
> and set forth the unity of your church,
> proclaim the Christian faith,
> maintain worship in spirit and in truth,
> feed the flock of Christ,
> and in all things care for your church.
>
> All this we ask through Jesus Christ,
> who lives with you and the Holy Spirit,
> one God, now and for ever.

People: **Amen.**

A psalm, hymn, or spiritual song is sung.

INAUGURATING A REGIONAL COVENANTING COUNCIL

Presentation

Leader: Dear friends in Christ, we now establish a Covenanting Council for our churches in (insert name of the place).

A representative of each church presents its members of the Covenanting Council.

Leader: These persons, whose names are before you, have been designated by their respective churches to serve as a Covenanting Council. They have accepted this call and are now here present in witness to their intention to serve.

The Charge:

Leader: You have been called together to serve the Church of Jesus Christ. In fulfilling your ministry you are to make effective the elements of our covenanting together toward the unity we seek. You are called to share in the responsibility for pastoral care of ordained ministers. You are charged to enable the covenanting churches to express more clearly evangelical and prophetic witness and service. You are to work within your own churches and together as a Council toward the development of personal and corporate spiritual disciplines. You are charged to be faithful to the churches' agreement that all our ordinations should manifest the covenantal nature of our communion. You are to serve with other Covenanting Councils — national, regional, and local — and to guide your churches through the covenanting journey, following the leading of Christ, who is the Shepherd of the flock.

Prayer to Affirm the Council

The prayer to affirm the Council is offered by a previously recognized and reconciled bishop.

Bishop: The Lord be with you.

People: **And with your spirit.**

Bishop: Let us pray.

Eternal God,
you have called these sisters and brothers
to serve you and your Church
through this covenanting council.
We thank you for the gifts
and grace they bring to the task.
Send your Holy Spirit upon them,
that they may serve faithfully and with diligence,
to the glory of your Name.

People: **Amen.**

Response of the People

Bishop: Dear friends, you have witnessed the constituting of this Covenanting Council. Therefore on their behalf, I ask you to pray for them to live in covenant in such a way as will more fully manifest the unity of Christ's Body. Will you support these members of the Covenanting Council, praying for them and their ministry within our community of faith?

People: **We will, with thanks to our God.**

Dismissal of the Covenanting Council

Bishop: We rejoice in the unity of which you as a Covenanting Council are a sign, and call upon you to enable our deepening covenant of love, service and witness. With you, we pledge ourselves to this journey, trusting that our Covenant God will lead us to that unity, visible and invisible, into which we are baptized.

Sisters and brothers of the Council, you may go in peace.

SERVICE OF THE TABLE

Offering

An Offering is received for the work of the Covenanting Council.

Preparing the Table of the Lord.

During the Offertory, newly installed members of the Covenanting Council bring to the altar gifts that represent the life and work of their respective churches. The elements for the Eucharist are brought to the Table of the Lord.

The Eucharist is then celebrated using the rite contained in the Sacrament of the Lord's Supper (1984), *beginning with the Great Thanksgiving.*

End of the Regional Service

A Local Service

**For Reaffirming Baptismal Vows,
Reconciling Presbyteral Ministers of Word and Sacrament,
Welcoming Ordained Deacons and
Ordained Ministers of Governance,
And Celebrating The Sacrament of The Lord's Supper**

OUTLINE OF THE SERVICE

INTRODUCTORY AND PENITENTIAL RITES
Processional Hymn
Acclamation
Declaration of Purpose
A Litany of Confession

LITURGY OF THE WORD
Prayer for Illumination
First Reading – Old Testament
Psalm
Second Reading – New Testament
Hymn
Gospel
Sermon

REAFFIRMATION OF BAPTISMAL PROMISES
Invitation
Renewal of Baptismal Covenant
Prayer over Water

PRAYERS OF THE PEOPLE

RECONCILING PRESBYTERAL MINISTERS OF WORD AND SACRAMENT, AND WELCOMING ORDAINED DEACONS AND ORDAINED MINISTERS OF GOVERNANCE
Processional Hymn
Statement of Purpose
Prayer

RECONCILING PRESBYTERAL MINISTERS OF WORD AND SACRAMENT
Presentation
Renewal of Vows
Prayer for the Wider Exercise of Ministry
Signs of Reconciliation

WELCOMING ORDAINED DEACONS AND ORDAINED MINISTERS OF GOVERNANCE
Presentation
Declaration of Intention
Renewal of Vows
Prayer for the Wider Exercise of Ministry
Signs of Welcome

INAUGURATING A REGIONAL COVENANTING COUNCIL
Presentation
The Charge
Prayer to Affirm the Council
Response of the People
Dismissal of the Covenanting Council

SERVICE OF THE TABLE
Offering
Preparing the Table of the Lord

A Local Service

For Reaffirming Baptismal Vows,
Reconciling Presbyteral Ministers of Word and Sacrament,
Welcoming Ordained Deacons and
Ordained Ministers of Governance,
And Celebrating The Sacrament of The Lord's Supper

INTRODUCTORY AND PENITENTIAL RITES

Processional Hymn

During the singing of this hymn, leaders of the service take their appointed places.

Acclamation

Bishop: Blessed be our God.

People: **For ever and ever. Amen.**

Declaration of Purpose

Bishop: We are gathered here as representatives of churches that are covenanting to become one people in worship, life and mission. Already our churches, through representative leaders, have declared their mutual recognition of one another, made covenant, and reconciled ministers with ordaining responsibility. They have created covenanting councils to foster further growth in unity at every level of the life of the churches. Now we have gathered to enter personally into this covenanted life by affirming our baptismal vows and by reconciling and welcoming the ministries of presbyters and welcoming ordained deacons and ordained ministers of governance who hitherto have functioned in the isolation of our respective churches.

A Litany of Confession

A leader: We come from many traditions, separated from one another by our expressions of the faith, but united because of our baptism into Christ. Let us confess the sin of our division and affirm the unity that God creates by our baptism into the death and resurrection of our Savior Jesus Christ. Dear friends, let us love one another, because love comes from God. Whoever loves is a child of God and knows God.

All sing: **Jesus Christ, the life of the world, and of all creation, forgive our separation and grant us peace and unity.**

Leader: The peace that Christ gives is to guide you in the decisions you make; for it is in this peace that God has called you into the one body.

All sing: **Jesus Christ, the life of the world, and of all creation, forgive our separation and grant us peace and unity.**

Leader: With his own body Jesus broke down the wall that separates the peoples. By dying on the cross Christ destroys the enmity and unites the races into one body. In union with Christ we too are being built together with all the others into a place where God lives through the Spirit.

All sing: **Jesus Christ, the life of the world, and of all creation, forgive our separation and grant us peace and unity.**

Leader: Do your best to preserve the unity which the Spirit gives by means of the peace that binds you together. There is one body, one spirit, just as there is one hope to which God has called you.

All sing: **Jesus Christ, the life of the world, and of all creation, forgive our separation and grant us peace and unity. Amen.**

LITURGY OF THE WORD

Prayer for Illumination

A leader of worship offers the following prayer:

Eternal God,
through the generations you have called a people

to hear your Word and to live a life of praise,
    sacrifice and service.
Now you have called us to be members of this great
    company of your saints.
Create in us the mind of Christ
who willingly gave himself for our salvation.
Stir up within us the power of the Holy Spirit
who strengthens us to live the Christian life.
Through our voices may your creative Word
    be spoken
so that sin is forgiven, separation overcome, and
    life together achieved.
Eternal God, may your name be praised,
now and for ever.

People: **Amen.**

First Reading – Old Testament

Reader: A reading from (name of the book).

After the reading the reader says:

The Word of God.

People: **Thanks be to God.**

Psalm

A psalm is sung. A period of silence may follow.

Second Reading – New Testament

Reader: A reading from (name of the book).

After the reading the reader says:

The Word of God.

People: **Thanks be to God.**

Hymn

A hymn, psalm, or spiritual song is sung.

Gospel

The Holy Scriptures are brought to the appointed place for the reading of the gospel.

Reader: The holy gospel of Jesus Christ according to (name of the book).

People: **Glory to you, O Christ.**

After the gospel, the reader says:

The gospel of Christ.

People: **Praise to you, O Christ.**

The Sermon

A psalm, hymn or spiritual song is sung.

REAFFIRMATION OF BAPTISMAL PROMISES

A leader of worship invites the members of the assembly to reaffirm their baptismal covenant.

Invitation

Brothers and sisters in Christ: in the sacrament of Holy Baptism our Lord Jesus Christ has received us and made us members of his body the Church. We share life in Christ and have been nourished at the Lord's Table. Let us this day renew the covenant of our baptism and commit ourselves to the responsibilities of our service to Christ.

Renewal of Baptismal Covenant

Leader: Do you now affirm your baptismal covenant?

People: **I do.**

Leader: Do you renounce all the forces of evil in whatever guise they present themselves?

People: **I do.**

Leader: Do you commit yourself to Jesus Christ and his service in the world?

People: **I do, and with God's grace I will follow him as my Lord and Savior.**

Leader: Do you believe in God?

People: **I believe in God, the Father almighty, creator of heaven and earth.**

Leader: Do you believe in Jesus Christ?

People: **I believe in Jesus Christ, God's only Son, our Lord, who was conceived by the power of the**

> **Holy Spirit,**
> **born of the Virgin Mary,**
> **suffered under Pontius Pilate,**
> **was crucified, died, and was buried;**
> **he descended to the dead.**
> **On the third day he rose again;**
> **he ascended into heaven,**
> **he is seated at the right hand of the Father,**
> **and he will come again to judge the living**
> > **and the dead.**

Leader: Do you believe in the Holy Spirit?

People: **I believe in the Holy Spirit,**
> **the holy catholic Church,**
> **the communion of saints,**
> **the forgiveness of sins,**
> **the resurrection of the body,**
> **and the life everlasting. Amen.**

Prayer over water

Bishop: *Lift up your hearts.*

People: **We lift them to the Lord.**

Bishop: Let us give thanks to the Lord our God.

People: **It is right to give our thanks and praise.**

Bishop: We thank you, O God, for this gift of water.

Here water may be poured into a font.

> In the beginning your Spirit hovered over the
> > waters of creation and brought forth life.
> Through the waters of the flood you cleansed
> > the world of sin
> and delivered Noah and his family to a new life.
> Through the waters of the Red Sea you led your
> > people Israel
> out of bondage into the land you promised.
> In the waters of Mary's womb Jesus was nurtured,
> and at the Jordan you proclaimed him as your
> > beloved Son.
> You call us to be your adopted children through
> > the waters of baptism,
> and from generation to generation you cleanse
> and bring us from death to life.

We now call upon you, O God, as we come to
      this water:
send your Holy Spirit to fill your church,
and unite it in love, joy, and peace.
Stir up that Spirit within us,
as we renew the vows of our baptism.
Empower us to do your work of reconciliation
until that day when you make all things new,
through Jesus Christ our Savior.

People: **Amen.**

*Water may be sprinkled toward the congregation as the following
words are spoken:*

Remember your baptism and be thankful.

PRAYERS OF THE PEOPLE

The following prayer of intercession is offered. A leader begins:

Holy Trinity, One God,
let your glory fill the world.

People: **All praise to you, God our Creator,
for by your Word and Spirit
you created the heavens and the earth,
filled them with life,
and declared everything good.**

**All praise to you, God our Redeemer,
for sending apostles, prophets, teachers,
      and martyrs,
inspired by your Spirit
to speak the word of life;
but especially for becoming fully human
      in Jesus Christ.**

**All praise to you, God our Helper,
as wisdom you inspire us to do the truth,
as power you strengthen us to do justice.**

Holy God, let your glory fill the world.

Leader: Sovereign God, hear our prayer
for the heavens and the earth,
created in beauty
but now languishing in sin.

People: **Stir up in us passion for the earth**
                 and its care.
                 Inspire us and all the peoples of the world
                 to respect and enjoy creation as you intend.

Leader: Merciful God, we pray for the human family
                 everywhere
             and especially those who suffer
             from poverty and oppression.

People: **Shape us and all other churches**
                 that we may continue the work
                 of Jesus Christ,
                 preaching good news and deliverance
                 and working for the coming of your
                 rule on earth.

Leader: God of justice, hear our prayer
                 for our churches.
             Make us to be a conscience to this nation.

People: **Make us witnesses to the vision**
                 of a society that is just and responsible.
                 Enable us to be healers of people
                 and institutions,
                 wounded in the struggle to live faithfully.
                 Help us express the gospel in daily life
                 until all creation proclaims your glory.

Leader: O God, Creator of heaven and earth,
             Redeemer of the world,
             Sanctifier of the faithful:

People: **Have mercy upon us**
                 and grant us your peace.
                 Holy, blessed, and glorious Trinity, One God,
                 let your glory fill the world.
                 To you be all praise and thanksgiving,
                 now and forever more.
                 Amen.

Here, after a Hymn and Benediction, a recess for a meal may be taken, or there may be a musical offering such as a Te Deum.

RECONCILING PRESBYTERAL MINISTERS OF
WORD AND SACRAMENT,
AND WELCOMING ORDAINED DEACONS,
AND ORDAINED MINISTERS OF GOVERNANCE

Processional Hymn

After all assemble again for worship, a hymn is sung during the procession of those who will preside and the ministers to be reconciled.

During the singing of this hymn, bishops and lay leaders lead the procession of presbyters, deacons, and ordained ministers of governance who are to participate in the liturgy of reconciliation and welcome.

Statement of Purpose

Bishop: We have renewed our baptismal promises and joined in common prayer for the world. We now come with the women and men who serve among us as ordained leaders of the church. We now ask God's blessing upon them in their ministries. We welcome them into the wider service that is now possible in churches that are reconciled to one another.

Prayer

Bishop: Let us pray.

Ever-faithful God,
in every time and place you have called
        courageous men and women
to speak your word, offer sacrifices,
        and minister to your people in your name.
Today we offer you our thankful praise
        for these leaders among us.
Especially do we give you thanks for the pastors
        and teachers,
and the deacons and ministers of governance
who witness to the gospel
and represent the faith in their work.
Rekindle in them zeal for the gospel,
love of the church,
and the strong desire to serve the people
        of the world.

Welcome them into the wider ministry
of these churches of Christ, covenanting together.
In the name of Jesus Christ we pray.

People: **Amen.**

RECONCILING PRESBYTERIAL MINISTERS OF WORD AND SACRAMENT

Presentation

*The presbyteral ministers of Word and Sacrament from the covenanting
churches come forward. Representatives of the participating churches
who present these ministers address the bishops:*

All Representatives:

We bring before you these ordained presbyters
who minister within the life and discipline
          of our respective churches.
They have studied the Word of God and the
          faith of the church
and have prepared themselves for public
          service in the church
in the name of Christ.
They have been examined and ordained by
          the laying on of hands and prayer.
They are now called to enter more fully
into the covenanting and reconciling
          communion
that is being created among us by the Spirit
          of God.

Renewal of Vows

Bishop: As Presbyters you have been ordained to serve among
the baptized members of the people of God as ministers
of Word and Sacraments. In this role you bear responsibility for the discipline of the church and are teachers
and preachers of the faith, so that the world may believe
and the church be renewed, equipped, and strengthened
in its ministry.

Do you here, in the presence of Christ and this congregation, renew your commitment to this ministry which
your have received?

Answer: I do, with God's help.

Bishop:	Will you then continue the life of Christian discipleship which began when you were baptized?
Answer:	I will, by God's help.
Bishop:	Do you affirm the covenant of unity which our churches are making with one another?
Answer:	I do, by God's help.
Bishop:	Do you renew your commitment to proclaim the Word of God and administer the sacraments of the New Covenant?
Answer:	I do, by God's help.
Bishop:	Will you be a faithful and zealous pastor and servant of those committed to your care in the name of Jesus Christ, the Good Shepherd?
Answer:	I will, by God's help.

Prayer for the Wider Exercise of Ministry

All Covenanting Presbyters:

> We give you thanks, O God,
>   for calling us into this new covenant.
> Complete in us your gifts,
> received and exercised in our separation,
> that we may now minister together
>   as presbyters in your church.
> Give us grace to preach your word with boldness,
> administer your sacraments with faith,
> and care for your church in unity and love,
> to the glory of your Name.
> All this we ask through Jesus Christ,
> who lives with you and the Holy Spirit,
> one God, now and for ever.

People: **Amen.**

A hymn invoking the Holy Spirit is sung.

Signs of Reconciliation

During the singing of this hymn, stations are formed,
each consisting of a bishop and a lay person. Each
presbyter goes to one of these stations to receive, first

*from the bishop and then from the lay person, the signs
of reconciliation for wider ministry. The sign of reconciliation given by the bishop is the placing of the hand
of blessing upon the head in silence. The sign of reconciliation given by the lay person is the hand of fellowship or the holy kiss.*

*As the reconciled presbyters return to their places,
they greet one another and other members of the assembly in the love, joy, and peace of Christ.*

A psalm, hymn, or spiritual song may be sung.

WELCOMING ORDAINED DEACONS AND ORDAINED MINISTERS OF GOVERNANCE

Presentation

*The ordained deacons and ordained ministers of gov-
ernance from the covenanting churches come forward.
Representatives of the participating churches who present these ministers address the bishops:*

All Representatives:
> We bring before you these deacons
> and ordained ministers of governance.
> They have studied the Word of God
> and the faith of the Church
> and have prepared themselves for service
>   in the Church in the name of Christ.
> They have been examined and ordained
> by the laying on of hands and prayer.
> They now present themselves
> because of their desire to enter more fully
> into the covenanting and reconciling
>   communion
> that is here being created by the Spirit
>   of God.

Declaration of Intention

Bishop: All of our churches engage in diaconal ministry; so
also all of our churches provide for the participation
of other persons in ecclesiastical governance, ordained
and unordained. Without presuming to reconcile these
ordained offices into a single ministry of service and
governance at this time, we now welcome these or-

dained ministers within the shared life of the covenant
communion of our churches, anticipating the day when
our growth in unity will make possible a full reconciliation of all these ordained ministers of the church.

Renewal of Vows

Another Bishop:

You have been ordained to serve your churches in their
order and mission in Christ. The covenanting churches
recognize that your ministries have been exercised in
a variety of ways. We now welcome you to your ministry within this covenant communion which is now coming into being.

Do you here, in the presence of Christ and of us as
representatives of his Church, renew your commitment
to the ministry you have received?

Answer: I do.

Bishop: Will you continue the life of Christian
              discipleship which began when you were
              baptized?

Answer: I will, by God's help.

Bishop: Do you affirm the covenant of unity which our
              churches are making with each other?

Answer: I do, by God's help.

Bishop: Will you renew your commitment to help the
              people of God in their worship, witness, and service?

Answer: I will, by God's help.

Prayer for the Wider Exercise of Ministry

All Covenanting Deacons and Ordained Ministers of Governance:

We give you thanks, O God,
for calling us into this new covenant.
Complete in us your gifts,
received and exercised in our separation,
that we may continue to be servants in
        pastoral care and governance,
and leaders of the church's mission
        in the world.

Give us grace that we may minister together
    in unity and love
that the world may know Jesus Christ.

All this we ask through him,
who lives with you and the Holy Spirit,
one God, now and for ever.

People: **Amen.**

A hymn invoking the Holy Spirit is sung.

Signs of Welcome

During the singing of this hymn, stations are formed, each consisting of a bishop and a lay person. Each ordained deacon and ordained minister of governance goes to one of these stations to receive, first from the bishop and then from the lay person, the signs of welcome into the wider ministry. The welcoming sign given by the bishop is the placing of the hand of blessing upon the head in silence. The welcoming sign given by the lay person is the hand of fellowship or the holy kiss.

As the welcomed deacons and ministers of governance return to their places, they greet one another and other members of the assembly in the love, joy, and peace of Christ.

A psalm, hymn, or spiritual song is sung.

INAUGURATING A LOCAL COVENANTING COUNCIL

Presentation

Leader: Dear friends in Christ, we now establish a Covenanting Council for our churches in (insert name of the place).

A representative of each church presents its members of the Covenanting Council.

Leader: These persons, whose names are before you, have been designated by their respective churches to serve as a Covenanting Council. They have accepted this call and are now here present in witness to their intention to serve.

The Charge

Leader: You have been called together to serve the Church of Jesus Christ. In fulfilling your ministry you are to

make effective the elements of our covenanting together toward the unity we seek. You are called to
share in the responsibility for pastoral care of ordained
ministers. You are charged to enable the covenanting
churches to express more clearly evangelical and
prophetic witness and service. You are to work within
your own churches and together as a Council toward
the development of personal and corporate spiritual
disciplines. You are charged to be faithful to the
churches' agreement that all our ordinations should
manifest the covenantal nature of our communion. You
are to serve with other Covenanting Councils — national, regional, and local — and to guide your
churches through the covenanting journey, following
the leading of Christ, who is the Shepherd of the flock.

Prayer to Affirm the Council

*The prayer to affirm the Council is offered by a previously recognized
and reconciled bishop.*

Bishop: The Lord be with you.

People: **And with your spirit.**

Bishop: Let us pray.

Eternal God,
you have called these sisters and brothers
to serve you and your Church
through this covenanting council.
We thank you for the gifts
and grace they bring to the task.
Send your Holy Spirit upon them,
that they may serve faithfully and with diligence,
to the glory of your Name.

People: **Amen.**

Response of the People

Bishop: Dear friends, you have witnessed the constituting of
this Covenanting Council. Therefore on their behalf,
I ask you to pray for them to live in covenant in such
a way as will more fully manifest the unity of Christ's
Body. Will you support these members of the Cove-

nanting Council, praying for them and their ministry within our community of faith?

People: **We will, with thanks to our God.**

Dismissal of the Covenanting Council

Bishop: We rejoice in the unity of which you as a Covenanting Council are a sign, and call upon you to enable our deepening covenant of love, service and witness. With you, we pledge ourselves to this journey, trusting that our Covenant God will lead us to that unity, visible and invisible, into which we are baptized.

Sisters and brothers of the Council, you may go in peace.

SERVICE OF THE TABLE

Offering

An Offering is received for the work of the Covenanting Council.

Preparing the Table of the Lord.

During the Offertory, newly installed members of the Covenanting Council bring to the altar gifts that represent the life and work of their respective churches. lThe elements for the Eucharist are brought to the Table of the Lord.

The Eucharist is then celebrated using the rite contained in the Sacrament of the Lord's Supper (1984), *beginning with the Great Thanksgiving.*

End of the Local Service

MEMBERSHIP OF THE DRAFTING COMMISSIONS

Church Order Commission
(Drafters of Part I)

Church Representatives

African Methodist Episcopal Church	The Rev. Daniel W. Jacobs, Sr.
African Methodist Episcopal Zion Church	Dr. Tecumseh X. Graham
Christian Church (Disciples of Christ)	Dr. Paul A. Crow, Jr., **Chair**
	The Rev. Dawn Kizzia Stemple
Christian Methodist Episcopal Church	Dr. William C. Larkin
Episcopal Church	The Rt. Rev. William G. Burrill
	The Rt. Rev. Andrew F. Wissemann
International Council of Community Churches	The Rev. Jane Ireland
	Dr. Robert H. Taylor
Presbyterian Church (U.S.A.)	Dr. George P. Morgan
	Elder Marianne Wolfe
United Church of Christ	Dr. William K. Laurie
United Methodist Church	The Rev. Vernon Bigler
	The Rev. Howell Wilkins

At Large Members

The Rt. Rev. John H. Burt
The Rev. Jeanne Audrey Powers
The Rev. Lewis L. Wilkins, Jr.

Advisory Consultants

Lutheran Council in the U.S.A.	Dr. Joseph A. Burgess
Reformed Church in America	The Rev. John Hiemstra
National Council of Churches	Dr. Kathleen Hurty
Roman Catholic Church	Professor Gerard Sloyan

Worship Commission
(Drafters of Part II)

Church Representatives

African Methodist Episcopal Church	Bishop Vinton R. Anderson, **Chair** The Rev. Cyrus S. Keller
African Methodist Episcopal Zion Church	Mr. Alfred Jarrett
Christian Church (Disciples of Christ)	Professor Keith Watkins
Christian Methodist Episcopal Church	Dr. Captolia Newbern
Episcopal Church	Professor Leonel Mitchell
International Council of Community Churches	The Rev. Ronald Miller Dr. Charles Trentham
Presbyterian Church (U.S.A.)	Professor Horace Allen, Jr. Dr. Lewis A. Briner Mrs. Lucille Hair
United Church of Christ	Ms. Dorothy M. Lester
United Methodist Church	Dr. Richard Eslinger Dr. Sharon Rhodes-Wickett

Advisory Consultants

Christian Church (Disciples of Christ)	The Rev. Peter Morgan
United Methodist Church	The Rev. Hoyt Hickman The Rev. Thomas A. Langford, III Dr. William D. Thompson
American Baptist Churches in the U.S.A.	
Lutheran Council in the U.S.A.	Dr. Joseph A. Burgess
Reformed Church in America	The Rev. James R. Esther
Roman Catholic Church	Monsignor Allen Detscher The Rev. Ronald Krisman

RELATED MATERIALS

The COCU Consensus: In Quest of a Church of Christ Uniting.
This 55-page document contains the theological basis for the covenanting plan. It is the companion text to *Churches in Covenant Communion*, and is an inherent part of the proposal.
                    PRICE: $1.25, plus $1.00 shipping and handling

Digest of the Proceedings of the Sixteenth Meeting of the Consultation on Church Union, Volume XVI (Baltimore, MD — 1984).
This 327-page document contains the complete record of the actions, reports, and participants in the Plenary assembly of the Consultation that approved and submitted to the churches The *COCU Consensus* for action.
                    PRICE: $10.00, plus $1.00 shipping and handling

Digest of the Proceedings of the Seventeenth Meeting of the Consultation on Church Union, Volume XVII (New Orleans, LA — 1988).
This document, when completed, will be of approximately the same length as the *Digest* of the Sixteenth Plenary (above). It is the official record of the Plenary that approved the proposal, *Churches in Covenant Communion*, and submitted it to the churches for action.
                    Anticipated publication date: April 30, 1989.
                    PRICE: $11.00, plus $1.00 shipping and handling

OTHER INTERPRETIVE RESOURCES

"The Essence of the COCU Covenanting Proposal": one-page leaflet. Single copies free. Quantities 5 cents each.

"What's It All About?": brief answers to twenty questions often asked about the Covenanting proposal. 25 cents each. Quantity discounts available.

Available from
                    Consultation on Church Union
                    Research Park – 151 Wall St.
                    Princeton, New Jersey 08540-1514

Phone (609) 921-7866

Orders totaling less than $10.00 must be prepaid. Larger orders may be invoiced.